AF292340

William Morris
at Middleton Cheney

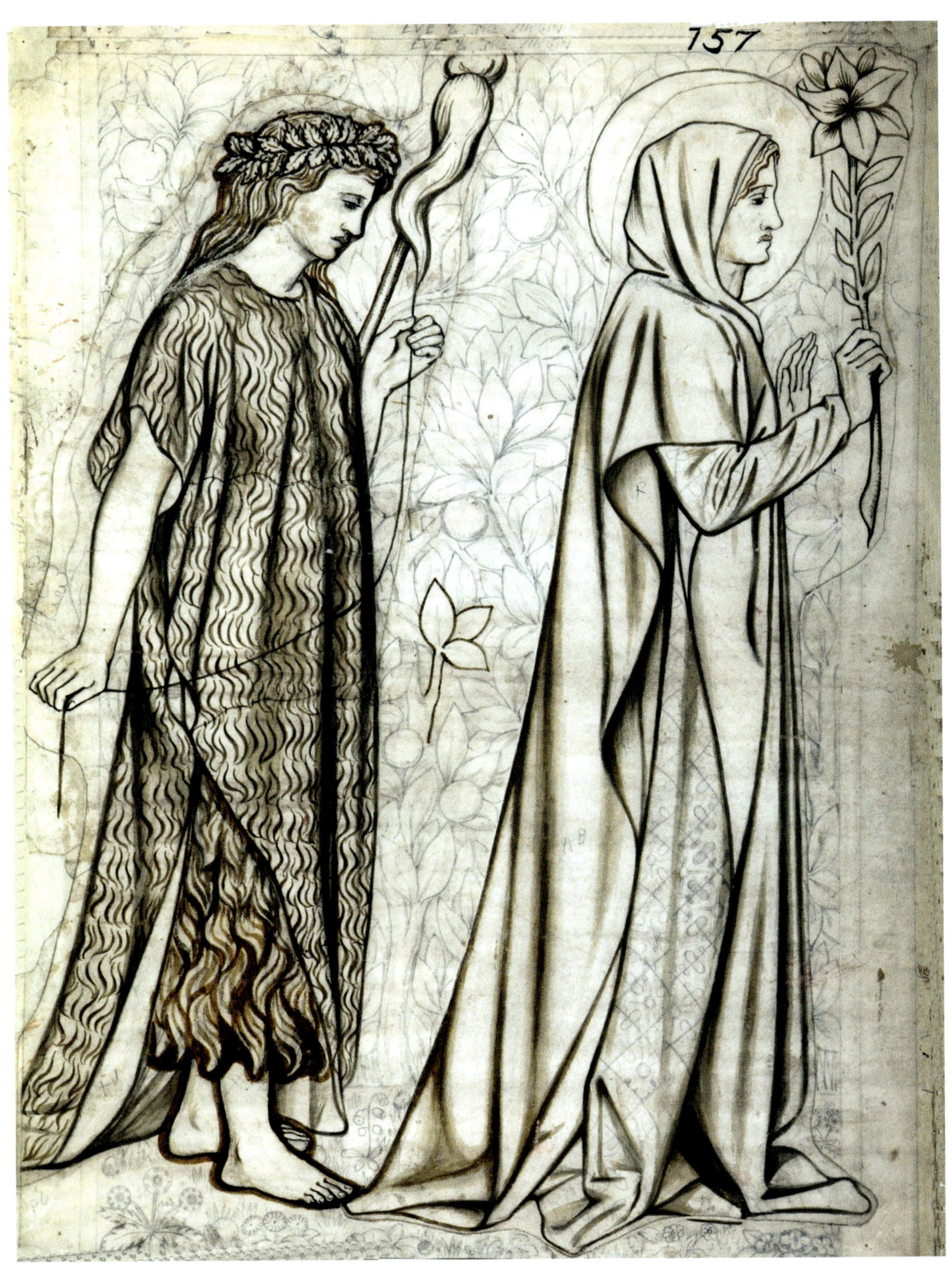

1864 cartoon for Eve and the Virgin by William Morris, for the west window of All Saints Church, Middleton Cheney (*see p. 20*) (*copyright © William Morris Gallery, London Borough of Waltham Forest*)

William Morris
at Middleton Cheney

The Stained Glass in All Saints Church

FIRCONE BOOKS

FRONT COVER: Detail of the east window at All Saints Church (1865), showing the figures of St Peter (a William Morris self-portrait) and St Paul (a portrait of Edward Burne-Jones).
BACK COVER: Detail of the west window (1871), showing three of the Six Days of Creation panels (numbers four, five and six).

First published in 2019 by Fircone Books Ltd.
The Holme, Church Road, Eardisley, HR3 6NJ
www.firconebooks.com

ISBN 978-1-907700-09-5

Text copyright © Richard Wheeler, David Thompson, Brian Goodey and Roger Bellamy
Images copyright © Richard Wheeler unless otherwise indicated

All rights reserved.
The moral right of the authors has been asserted.

Without limiting the rights under copyright reserved above, no part of this publication may be reproduced, stored in or introduced into a retrieval system, or transmitted, in any form or by any means (electronic, mechanical, photocopying, recording or otherwise), without prior written permission of the copyright owner and the above publisher of this book.

Designed and typeset by Richard Wheeler.
Cover design by Richard Wheeler.

Printed and bound in Malta

Fircone Books is committed to a sustainable future for our business, our readers and our planet.
The book in your hands is made from paper certified by the Forest Stewardship Council.

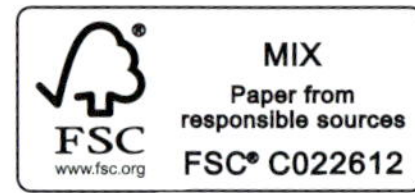
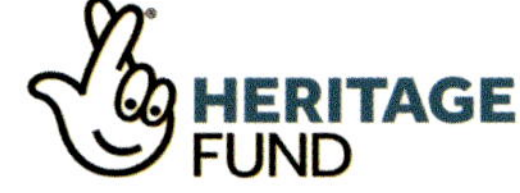

British Library Catalogue in Publishing Data.
A CIP catalogue record for this book is available from the British Library.

CONTENTS

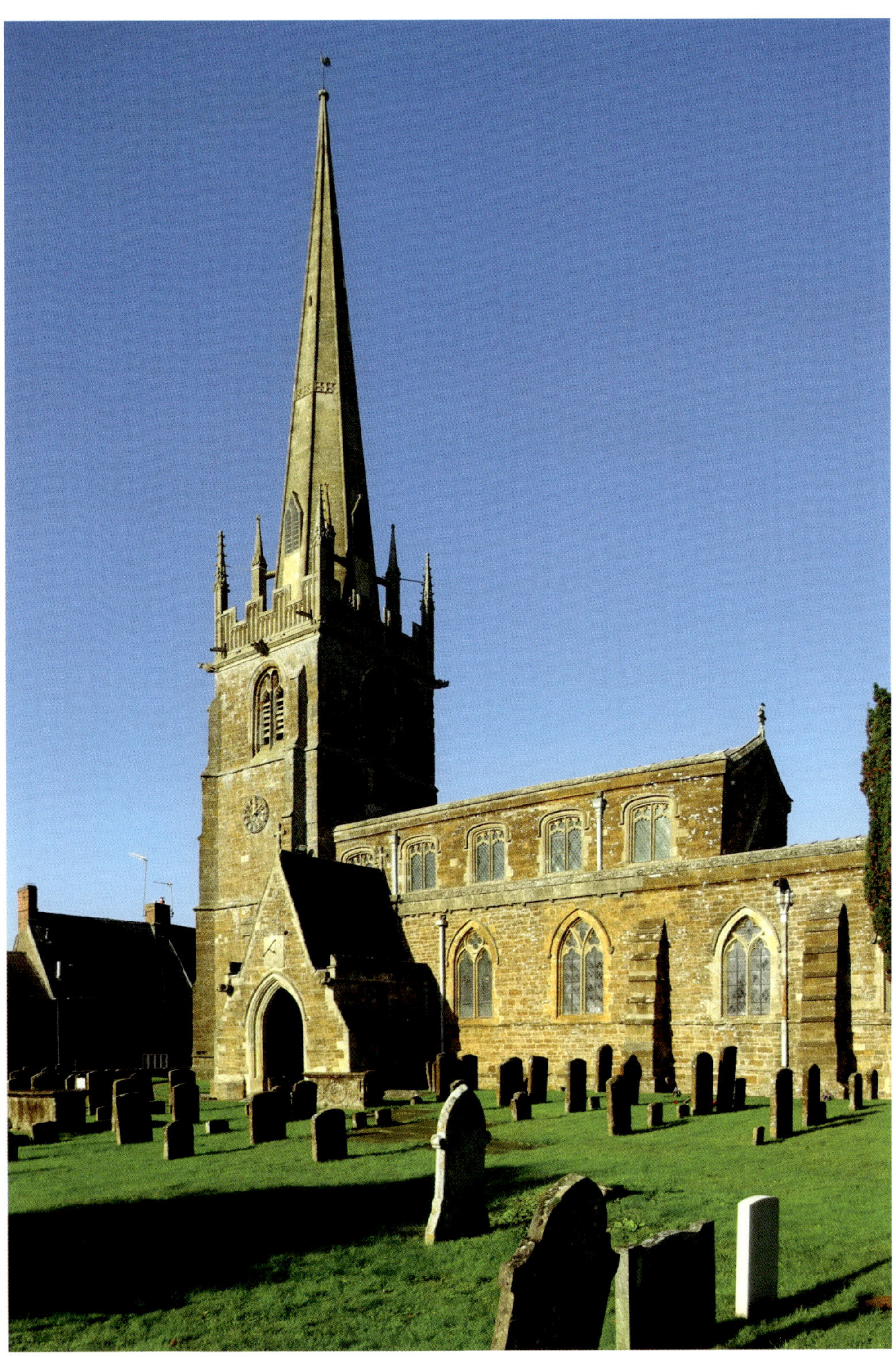

PREFACE AND ACKNOWLEDGEMENTS

All Saints is the much-loved parish church of the village of Middleton Cheney in Northamptonshire, sited close to the Oxfordshire border. Dating from the late 1200s, it was an early part of a wave of church building across England between 1300 and 1350. It is famous for its stained glass windows by Morris & Co., and there is also a painted roof scheme by Morris dating from 1865.

Between 2008 and 2014 the church had lead stolen from its roof three times, with significant damage to the interior caused by the ingress of rainwater. The nave roof had been extensively repaired in 1865, but not re-covered since then. Hairline cracks had appeared on the sunny south aspect of the roof, caused by the repeated expansion and contraction of the lead. By 2010 the roof had begun to leak, its weaknesses being exploited by more frequent intense rainfall events. In 2014 Historic England placed it on the Register of Places of Worship at Risk, by virtue of the state of the roof and its rainwater goods.

For these reasons, despite patching, it became imperative to re-cover the roof, to make the building watertight again and to preserve its artistic heritage. In 2018 we were very fortunate in being awarded, by the National Lottery Heritage Fund, a substantial grant towards the cost of the works. Historic England supported our case for re-covering the roof with terne coated steel rather than lead, as a deterrent against future roof metal theft.

If it were not for the National Lottery Heritage Fund this book would never have been published. They provided both the financial support and impetus for a number of people – in particular members of the All Saints regular congregation and villagers of Middleton Cheney who love the building – to pool their knowledge about the church's architectural and artistic heritage. Researching the history of a church for publication is no easy undertaking. Despite the vast amount of information now available on the internet, the process requires much checking of original sources, the resolution of contradictions by cross-checking

– and the curiosity to ask questions, the answers to which will hopefully reveal further insights into our country church. When assembling information for such a book it is particularly important to know when to stop. The side alleys invariably lead into the depths of local social history, national history, the history of art, architectural practice and theology. The story is about people rather than just stone and glass.

Why publish a book about William Morris and the involvement of his two companies between 1865 and 1893 in the decoration – particularly the stained glass – of All Saints, Middleton Cheney? A simple answer is that the glass is beautiful and evokes an emotional response in all who see it. It is also the case that the stained glass here is nationally important, comprising an early and complete set of windows by some of the foremost artists and designers of the day, and together representing one of the finest collections of Victorian stained glass to survive anywhere. This has made the church famous amongst those interested in Pre-Raphaelite art and the Arts and Crafts movement. Over six decades it has featured in a series of guide books, including: Nikolaus Pevsner's *Buildings of England* (1961); Simon Jenkins' *England's Thousand Best Churches* (1999), and Paul Sharpling's *Fragile Images* (2016). However, the church – and specifically its glass – has never been the subject of the dedicated study called for by Pevsner more than 50 years ago, when he wrote of the stained glass at All Saints, 'It is so beautiful and so important that it deserves a detailed record'.

All Saints church sits on two long-distance footpaths, and although walkers often call in, sometimes knowing little about churches or stained glass, it is noticeable what an impact the windows have, many staring in awe at what they are seeing within a modest rural church. One of the greatest virtues of stained glass is its ever-changing appearance as the daylight changes, enhanced by our very variable weather in the UK. The colours in the east window exploit the rising sun, and in the west window its setting.

Naturally, the church also attracts visitors who come specifically to look at the glass (and some to photograph it), but before this publication we had little printed information readily available to satisfy this interest (aside from our series of short church guides). Hopefully this book meets that need. Increasing interest in All Saints – partly as a result of this book – has also contributed to its presence online, and the ability of people across the world to learn more about the church and its stained glass.

Morris would have been pleased.

In addition to the substantial grant from the National Lottery Heritage Fund towards the re-covering of the roof, the All Saints PCC would like to gratefully thank the following donors: the National Churches Trust; Northamptonshire Historic Churches Trust; Banbury United Charities, and the Jill Franklin Trust.

Numerous people in Middleton Cheney got behind the fundraising effort for the project; the WI ran a mammoth jumble sale and organised a concert; the Middleton Cheney Singers choir ran a series of concerts, and many people baked cakes and made coffee.

Richard Wheeler, photographer, for his stunning images of the windows and other features of the church. Fircone Books Ltd., publishers of books on church architecture, for putting the book together. Their skills, expertise, knowledge and ability to liaise constructively with a range of people were appreciated.

Irene Forrest, former churchwarden, who produced the original church guide (1994) which provided the basis for continuing research. In this she was assisted by David Shackleton, former churchwarden. Bob Hunter, a congregational member, who has continued the research into the history of the church building and sought interpretations of it for over 30 years. Brian Goodey, Emeritus Professor at the School of Architecture at Oxford Brookes University – a village resident, who generously shared his research findings on the building, particularly the windows. Nancy Long, the Honorary Village Archivist, who dug with much enthusiasm into newspaper archives and records contained in the Northamptonshire Record Office. Sue Hunter, congregational member, for her checks on theological accuracy and her editorial comments. Bridget Robb and Mike Wilks, churchwardens, for their enthusiasm for the publication of this book and the editing of drafts. David Thompson, former churchwarden, for his work in fundraising and bringing to fruition the project to re-cover the roof.

Bryan Martin, the supervising conservation architect, for bringing to bear his expertise in repairing church roofs, not to mention his commitment to this project and passion for historic buildings. Shaun Ward of Prestige Metal Roofing, for his project management and craftsmanship in creating a steel roof of high quality, worthy of a Grade-I Listed church.

While putting together our grant bid to the National Lottery, the Revd Canon Roger Bellamy from nearby Kings Sutton offered to write a broad, personal Christian interpretation of the windows at All Saints to go into this book. Sadly, Roger died before completing his manuscript. Sue Hunter kindly agreed to complete it. We include Roger's essay here in this book, in his memory.

Revd Nick Leggett and All Saints PCC

Plan of All Saints Church, Middleton Cheney

(stained glass windows numbered chronologically in RED)

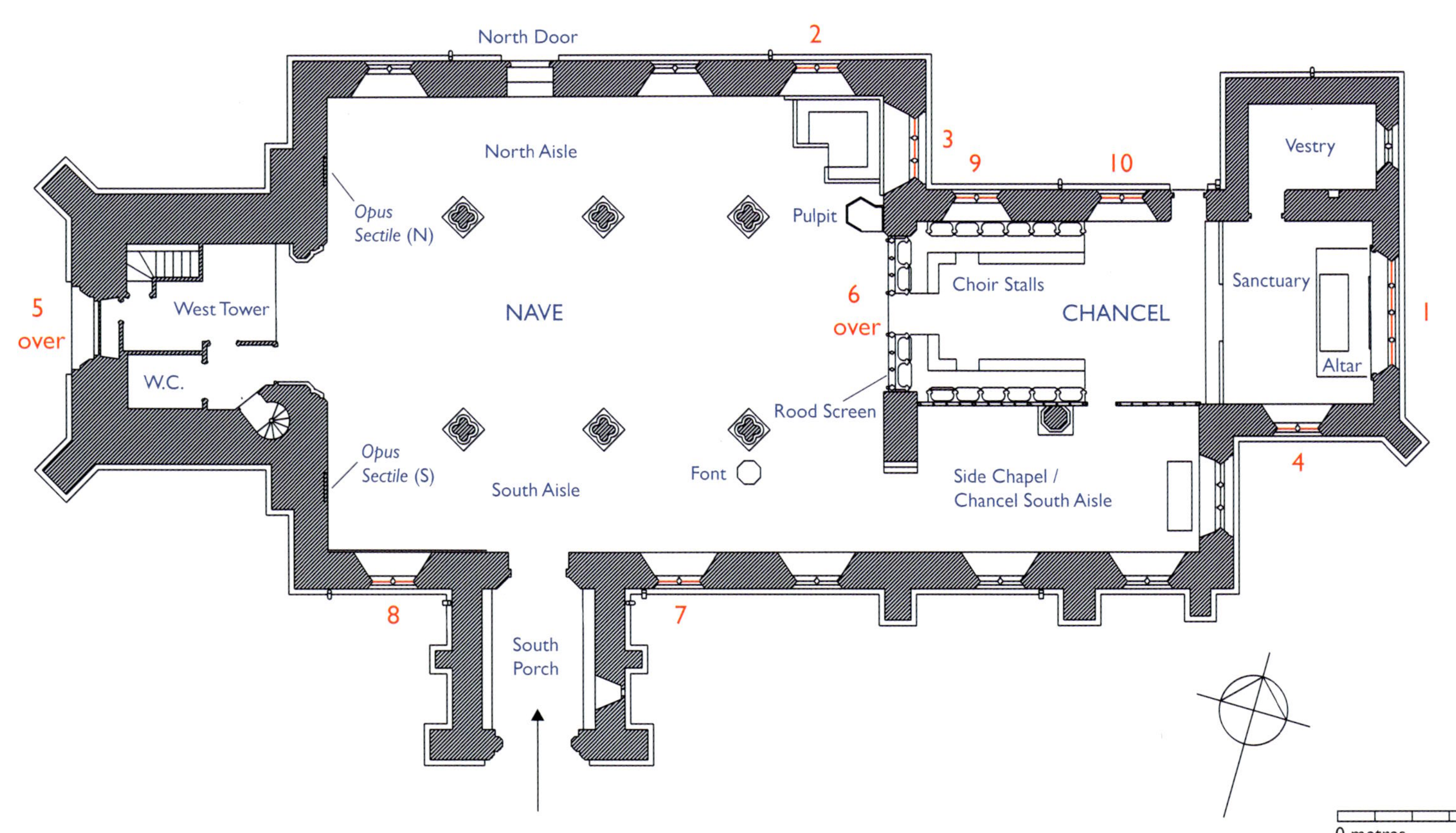

1

All Saints Church, Middleton Cheney

ALL Saints Church stands at the heart of Middleton Cheney, in a raised, triangular churchyard bounded by ironstone houses and cottages dating mainly from the seventeenth and eighteenth centuries. The earliest archaeological finds in the area include the remains of late Neolithic and early Bronze Age cremations discovered in the bounds of the village.

The earliest historical record for Middleton Cheney is contained in the Domesday Book (1086), which records a priest living in the village. Further documentary evidence can be found in the records of the Court of Arches, Canterbury, dated 1296. This concerns a dispute between an incoming rector and his predecessor relating to the dereliction and lack of maintenance of the old church. For the church to be in such a rundown state at this time may indicate that a church occupied this site as early as the late 1100s. However, no stonework or structure remain from this date (save, just possibly, for the two head corbels inside the south porch, and a further head set into the north wall of the north aisle). The earliest priest listed in church records, Radulphus de Middleton, served between 1180 and 1205.

Documentary evidence suggests that work on the medieval church was undertaken in two stages. The chancel was completely rebuilt following the Court of Arches' decision of 1296. The new nave was started sometime after 1302, with at least some of the building work taking place during the Rectorship of William de Edington (1322–35), the future Bishop of Winchester (responsible for the Cathedral's spectacular west front).

All Saints Church consists of a clerestoried nave with side aisles and a south porch, a chancel with a north vestry and south chapel (essentially an extension eastwards of the nave aisle before 1701, subsequently used as a church school until about 1831), and a west tower and spire. The fabric dates primarily from the first half of the fourteenth century, but with significant additions from the late fifteenth century and the nineteenth century. Reflecting the two principal medieval phases of building activity, the church predominantly derives its architectural character from the Decorated and Perpendicular phases of English Gothic.

While the church is justly celebrated for its collection of Pre-Raphaelite stained glass (discussed in detail in the following sections) it has many other features of interest – both in terms of its architecture and its fixtures and fittings.

The Victorian programme of works, carried out for Revd William Buckley and overseen by the architect George Gilbert Scott (and later by his son, George Gilbert Scott Junior) was begun in 1864. This entailed a major and relatively sympathetic restoration and re-ordering of the church which, according to the *Oxford Times* of 22 April 1865, 'had fallen into a sad and discreditable state of dilapidation'. Extensive repairs were carried out to the stonework, including the renewal of much of the window tracery, in readiness for the defining addition of the Morris & Co. stained glass. Inside, the box-pews and balconies in place at the time were removed, as were layers of whitewash; and the nave and chancel were refurnished. The success of the work owes much not only to Buckley's acquaintance with Scott, but also to his claimed acquaintance with Edward Burne-Jones, whose west window is one of the glories of the church.

Morris's work at Middleton Cheney, particularly with regards to the painted roof, represents one of his earliest forays into church restoration; though it is possibly predated by his work at All Saints Church, Coddington, near Newark-on-Trent, whose roof he also painted while working there in 1864–65.

EXTERIOR

Externally, the interest of the church is both architectural and sculptural.

The late fifteenth century saw the rebuilding of the tower, and the addition of the current spire. While Middleton Cheney's spire is less rich in sculpted detail than those at nearby Kings Sutton or Bloxham, it remains a handsome and effective composition in a part of the country rich in good spires. It shares with Kings Sutton a pair of pinnacles at each angle of the tower and a 'collar' of blind tracery (relief carving) encircling the spire itself; and with Bloxham a 'hollis', or gallery (here crenelated and blind-traceried) at the top of its tower. Also up there, thrusting out to all points of the compass, are strongly-modelled gargoyles (figurative water spouts) with gaping mouths.

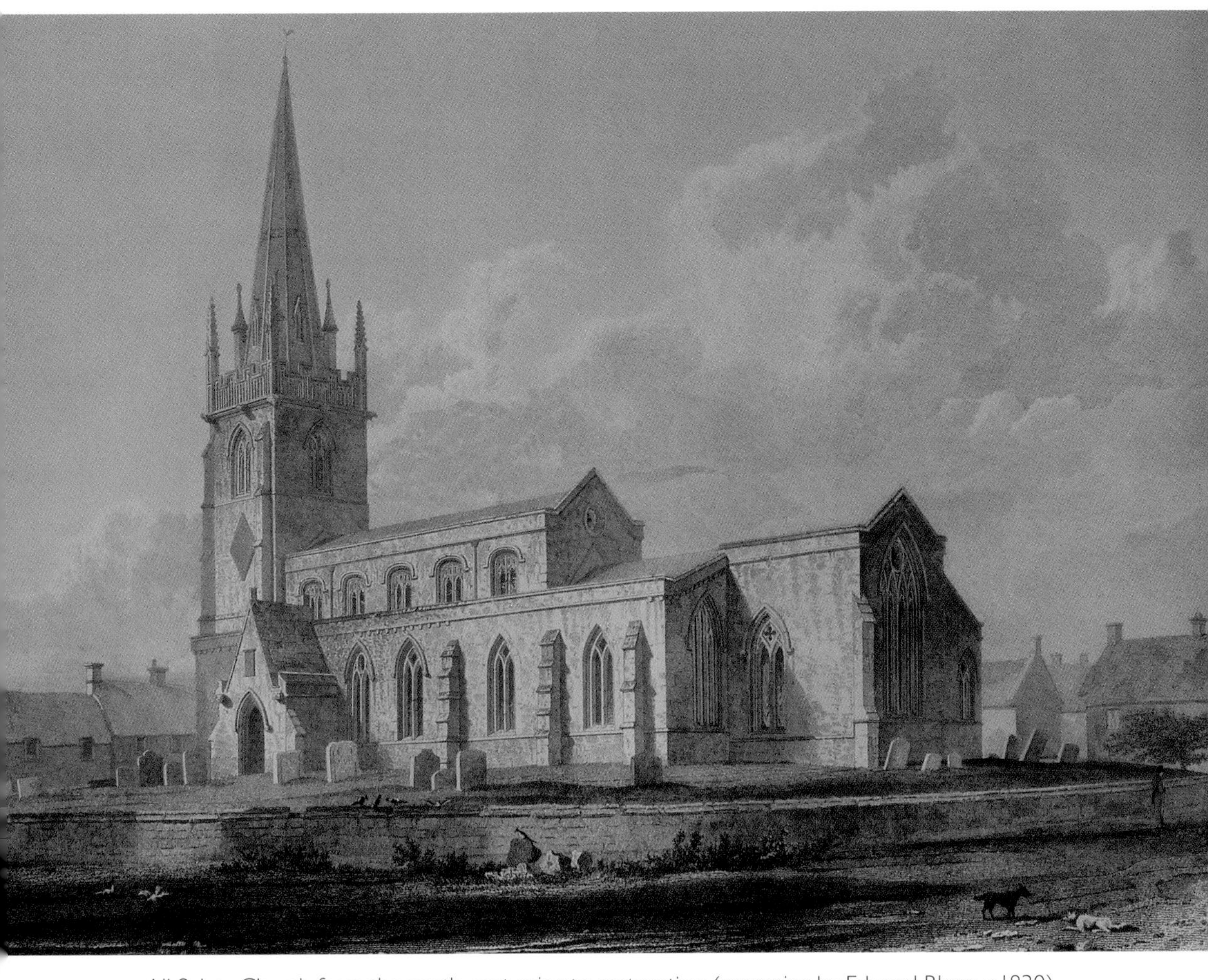

All Saints Church from the south-east prior to restoration (engraving by Edward Blore, c.1830)

The much-eroded west doorway also belongs to this period. Here, as well as an elaborately-moulded entrance arch, the spandrels between this and the containing rectangle have been filled with a depiction of the Annunciation. The Blessed Virgin Mary occupies the left-hand canopied niche; the Archangel Gabriel (wing outstretched) the right-hand niche, and there are four shield-bearing angels above. A possible local inspiration for this narrative treatment of a west doorway can be found at nearby Bloxham, whose earlier portal features a sculpted representation of the Last Judgment.

Other sculpture can be found along the north and south eaves of the side aisles, 'supporting' the parapet. The cornice here is studded with a gallery of heads, human and animal. The display of architectural sculpture here echoes (albeit on a more modest scale) that found on other nearby churches, including Bloxham, Adderbury and Hanwell; and the earlier corbel-tables (arrays of carved stones at eaves level) found on many Norman churches, including Cassington to the south, and the unfinished example at Iffley on the southern edge of Oxford.

The south porch is the most striking architectural feature of the church, and is highly unusual. It has a steeply-pitched gabled form, its triangular geometry deliberately accentuated by the roof line being carried down below the eaves by the buttresses flanking the outer doorway. The roof of the porch – laid with stone slabs rather than tiles – is supported inside, with great ingenuity, by a transverse arch infilled above with a stack of chunky, cusped tracery, and terminating in a pair of characterful head corbels. There is a similar, though smaller and less bold, south porch at nearby Chacombe (this too has a roof supported inside by transverse arches).

The south doorway, sheltering inside the south porch (and thus not subject to the weathering suffered by the west doorway), belongs to the early fourteenth-century. It is finely moulded, the central mouldings springing from attached shafts typical of the period, and with an overarching hood-mould with worn label-stops in the form of human heads. The north doorway and window tracery, excluding that of the clerestory (the upper level of the nave), also belong to this period. The north doorway, being originally a secondary entrance, is more simply-moulded than the south. The renewed windows contain tracery (known as 'Y' and 'intersecting' tracery) characteristic of the Geometric phase of Decorated Gothic, *c.*1260–1320. The ten clerestory side windows belong to the fifteenth century.

INTERIOR

More high quality and characteristic Decorated work of the fourteenth century can be found inside. The nave arcades are of four bays, the piers comprising four clustered shafts (thus giving a quatrefoil section) topped with finely-moulded capitals. The finesse of the arcades is also evident in the arches. Double-chamfered, pointed arches are a feature of many fourteenth-century nave arcades in the churches of this region (and further afield); however, here the outer chamfer is hollow-moulded, with the profile of the shaft and capital below dying into the ends of each arch. In a pattern common to other local churches of the period, the arches themselves are formed with alternating bands of darker and lighter stone.

The westernmost nave pier of the south arcade features a number of intriguing motifs scratched into the stonework. They are not easy to make out. Arguably the most interesting one comprises a circle containing six compass-drawn 'petals', symmetrically arranged. One might expect to find four (rather than six) petals arranged to form a Consecration Cross, but the additional petals give this the 'daisy wheel' form of a witches' mark (a secular mark applied to stonework and woodwork to ward off witches). Scratched over the top of this is a simpler Consecration Cross, and below this a pattern of overlapping rectangles. There is further graffiti on the easternmost pier of the north arcade (below the Morris head corbel, *see below*) in the form of two further Consecration Crosses.

As with the exterior, the wall surfaces inside are enlivened with figurative sculpture – some 100 examples, most in the form of corbels and label-stops, and encompassing a range of figures real or imagined. Some are taken from the Bestiary, including a basilisk or cockatrice with a curling tail, a grinning crocodile with a mouth full of teeth, and a green man. Others reference the actual and the living, including a bear with a rope around his muzzle (symbol of the Earls of Warwick) and a gallery of human heads, some pulling faces. The variations in features and headwear of the human heads make it possible that at least some of these were drawn from life – perhaps from those who worked on the church or lived in the village (as was the case with some of the corbels in Burford church in Oxfordshire). While many of the carvings are medieval, some are later, including one dated 1611 at the edge of the bell-ringing gallery. One head that almost certainly was taken from life is that occupying the easternmost pier of the north arcade: that of William Morris, added in *c*.1866.

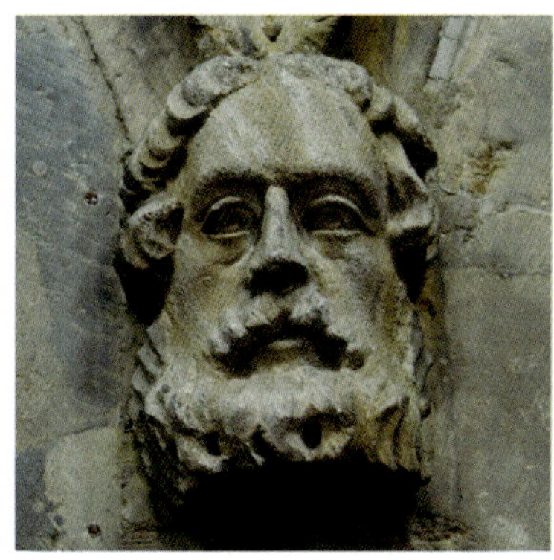

The William Morris head corbel

High up in the walls at the west ends of both side aisles are blocked windows containing *opus sectile* panels (a type of mosaic). Both windows were blocked up and covered over when buttresses were added to the north and south sides of the tower in the fifteenth century – only to be uncovered (though not unblocked) during the Victorian restoration of the church in the late nineteenth century. The panels are by the firm of James Powell and Sons at Whitefriars Glass, working closely with William Morris.

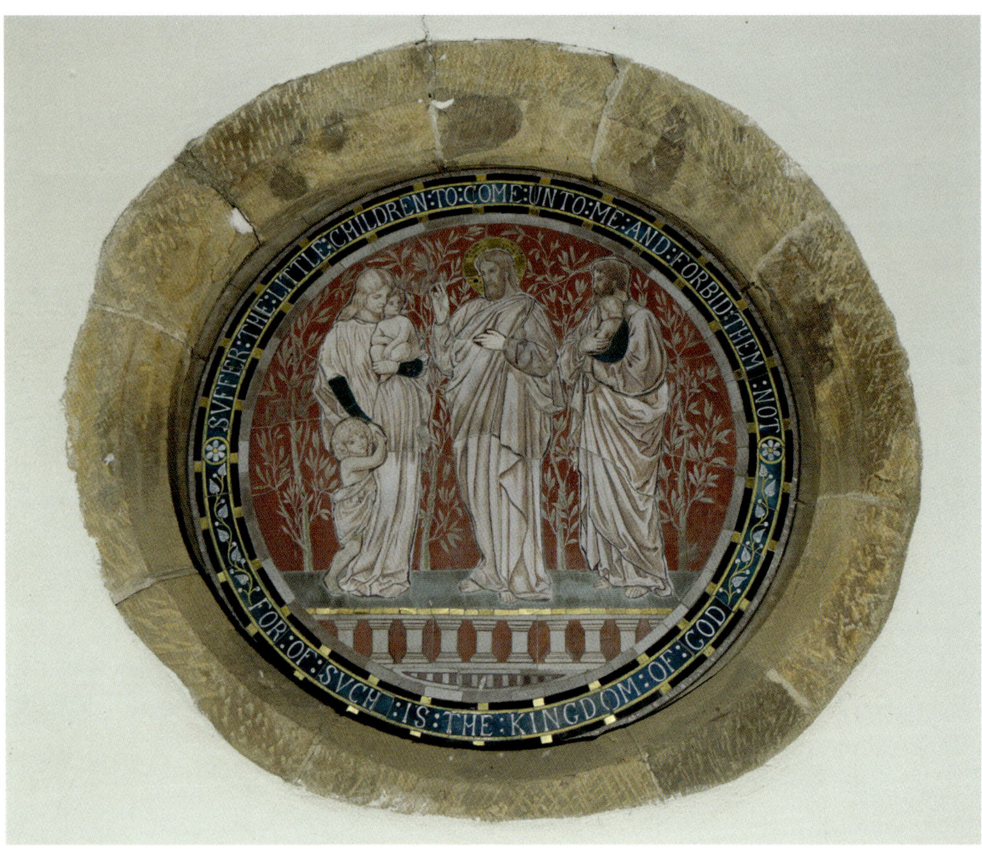

Opus Sectile (mosaic) roundel in the west wall of the south aisle, depicting Jesus and the Children

The south aisle mosaic roundel depicts Jesus and the Children, and is taken from a drawing by Henry Holiday. Holiday worked for Powell and Sons, and was also responsible for designing the spectacular scheme of mosaics and stained glass that makes a jewel box of the south transept of Buckland church in south Oxfordshire. (Holiday was also responsible for the illustrations in Lewis Carroll's *The Hunting of the Snark*).

The more highly coloured mosaic in the north aisle depicts the Sermon on the Mount, and is by Charles Hardgrave who, like Holiday, designed mosaics and stained glass while working for Powells. This panel is noteworthy for its use of small, gold-coloured glass rectangles, an innovation by Harry Powell who trained at Oxford as a chemist.

At the front of the north aisle is the Horton family pew. This is unusual, in that it post-dates the time when family pews were generally installed in churches. It signifies the arrival of Mary Ann Horton in the local community.

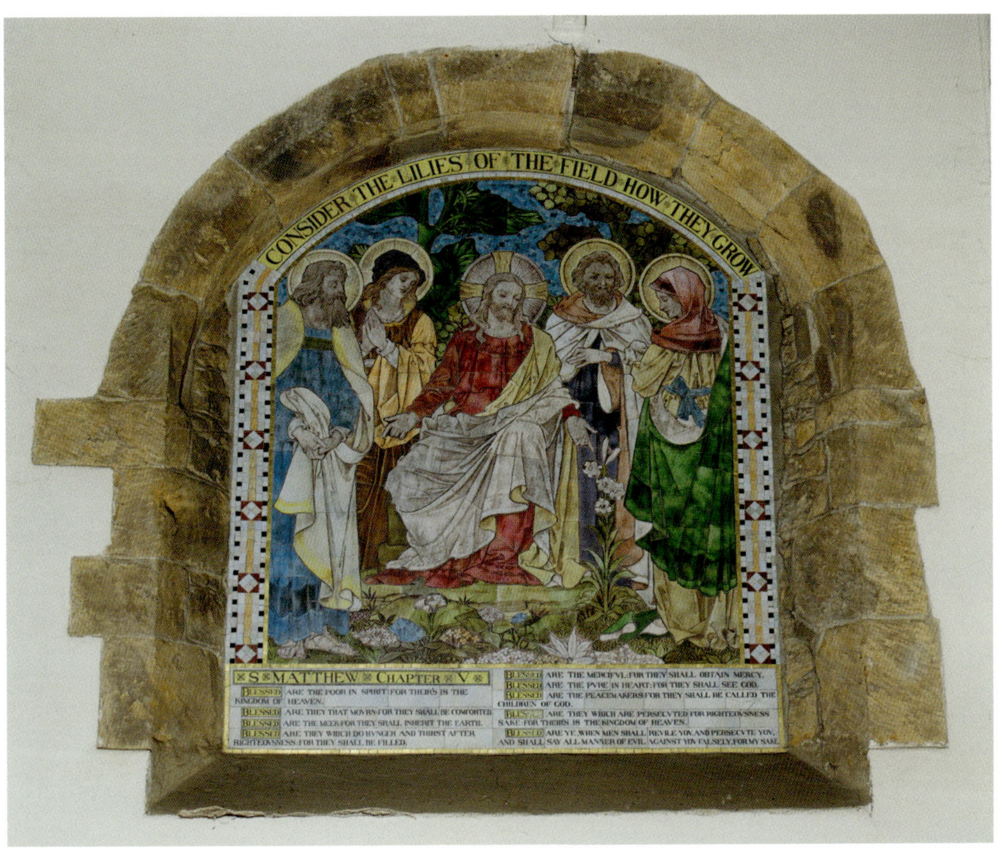

Opus Sectile (mosaic) panel in the west wall of the north aisle, depicting the Sermon on the Mount

The nave is partitioned from the chancel beyond by a rood-screen ('rood' from the Saxon word 'rodd' meaning a cross) dating from the second half of the fifteenth century or the first quarter of the sixteenth. This is a notable survival, being one of only a tiny handful of late medieval rood-screens still standing in Northamptonshire. The screen is largely original, with the projecting upper parts a not entirely successful legacy of Scott's restoration. The screen would originally have been fan-vaulted, with the vaulting springing both from the crowned caps of the outermost attached shafts (known as *bouttel* shafts) and those fronting the door-posts. With the loss of the original vaulting, Scott appears to have taken the decision to offset the blankness of the previously concealed spandrels of the main lights by infilling these with foliage-carved panels. He did the same with the spandrels in the door-head of the screen, perhaps feeling that the much bolder tracery of the ogee-headed doorway was at odds with the more delicate tracery of the flanking lights. (It is quite possible that the door-head belongs to an earlier screen, of fourteenth-century date, whose outer lights were updated in *c.*1500).

The screen was moved a short distance to the west during the re-ordering of 1865 (though almost certainly would have originally occupied its current position). This was done to make space for the new choir stalls, based on those at Brasenose College, Oxford, which has held the patronage of the church since 1693. It appears that the screen was once surmounted by a rood-loft, or at least a platform, unusually accessed by wooden steps from the south side of the nave (rather than the more common means of a mural stairwell from the chancel).

By looking closely at the screen, traces of the original paintwork can still be seen – for example, spiralling up the moulded shafts of the door-posts. Medieval rood-screens were generally decorated using a fairly limited palette consisting of red, green, blue, white and gold in the form of gilding. As part of the intended Victorian scheme of restoration, the screen was to be repainted (as was carried out, for example, on the medieval screen in nearby Bloxham church); however, the planned repainting of the All Saints' screen was never carried out. The pulpit to the left of the screen also dates from the fifteenth century, and was moved here from the north arcade in 1865. According to Revd Buckley, the pulpit was, 'examined with scrupulous care, and re-painted in the old colours, and pattern exactly.'

Other surviving medieval woodwork in the nave includes the south door, with its smaller 'wicket' door to restrict drafts and control access; the big, thickly-boarded chest which is thought to date from the fourteenth century and may have been a coffer for the building fund at this time; and a number of the benches at the west end of the nave, which are fifteenth-century and relatively plain, with a simple trefoil-section moulded rail (restored by Scott in the 1860s).

Further early woodwork survives in the roof. During the 1865 restoration of the nave roof, structural timbers (including sections of the tie beams) were preserved from the medieval roof, and reused. The tie beam over the chancel arch is painted with a representation of the head of Jesus in the centre, flanked by six of his Disciples. The remaining trusses are adorned with images of lions. The Last Supper and the lions have been carefully examined and were probably painted in the late fifteenth century. The remaining six Disciples – three on each end of the easternmost beam – were painted in about 1866 when the rotted ends of the beam had to be replaced.

The internal painting of the nave and chancel roofs was only recently recognised as being the work of Morris. The William Morris Society was in possession of the original designs, but the location of the finished work had never previously been identified. The designs comprise golden or red Tudor roses and propeller-like six-petalled flowers on the boarding; stencilled white flowers, undulating trails of foliage and spiralling (or 'barber's pole') decoration on the rafters and trusses, and an angular ribbon design on the purlins. The painting was carried out in 1865 by Mr Cottam, a painter and gilder from nearby Banbury.

In a paper of 1865, Revd Buckley recorded that:

> The nave roof has been coloured on the old patterns, and as far as could be ascertained in the old colours, on the ridge pieces, purlins and tie-beams, and spandrels of the braces. The rafters were in the old roof coloured red, such as were left. They are now red and yellow alternately, and the pattern on the roofing boards is new, nothing of any old pattern being visible. The chancel roof was renewed about the end of the last, or beginning of this century [i.e. 1800], and nothing of the olden roof was preserved. The colouring, therefore, was designed in accordance with the nave, but fuller of design and richer of colour.

Setting aside its painted ceiling and gallery of stained glass, the chancel is a relatively unadorned space. The only Decorated feature of note is the piscina (stone basin) in the south wall, with a triangular hood with leaf carving, topped with a crocketed (budding) finial. A much plainer piscina, this one with a pointed-arch head, survives in the south wall of the vestry, located behind the aumbry (recessed cabinet or cupboard) visible in the north wall of the chancel.

The other fixtures and fittings in the chancel are Victorian or later. The green and yellow floor tiles in the sanctuary are by the firm of William Godwin of Lugwardine, Herefordshire (a major manufacturer of the period). According to Revd Buckley, the designs are based on those of earlier encaustic tiles discovered while excavating around the foundations of the church. The chancel stalls and the parclose screen on the south side of the chancel were also added in the 1860s, as was the altar cloth and frontal. The 100 embroidered cushions and kneelers throughout the church are the result of a seven-year project initiated in 1990 by churchwarden Irene Forrest. The designs were prepared by her artist sister Joyce Christie, and are drawn from features of the church, including the Morris & Co. windows.

OVERLEAF: View of the painted nave roof looking east

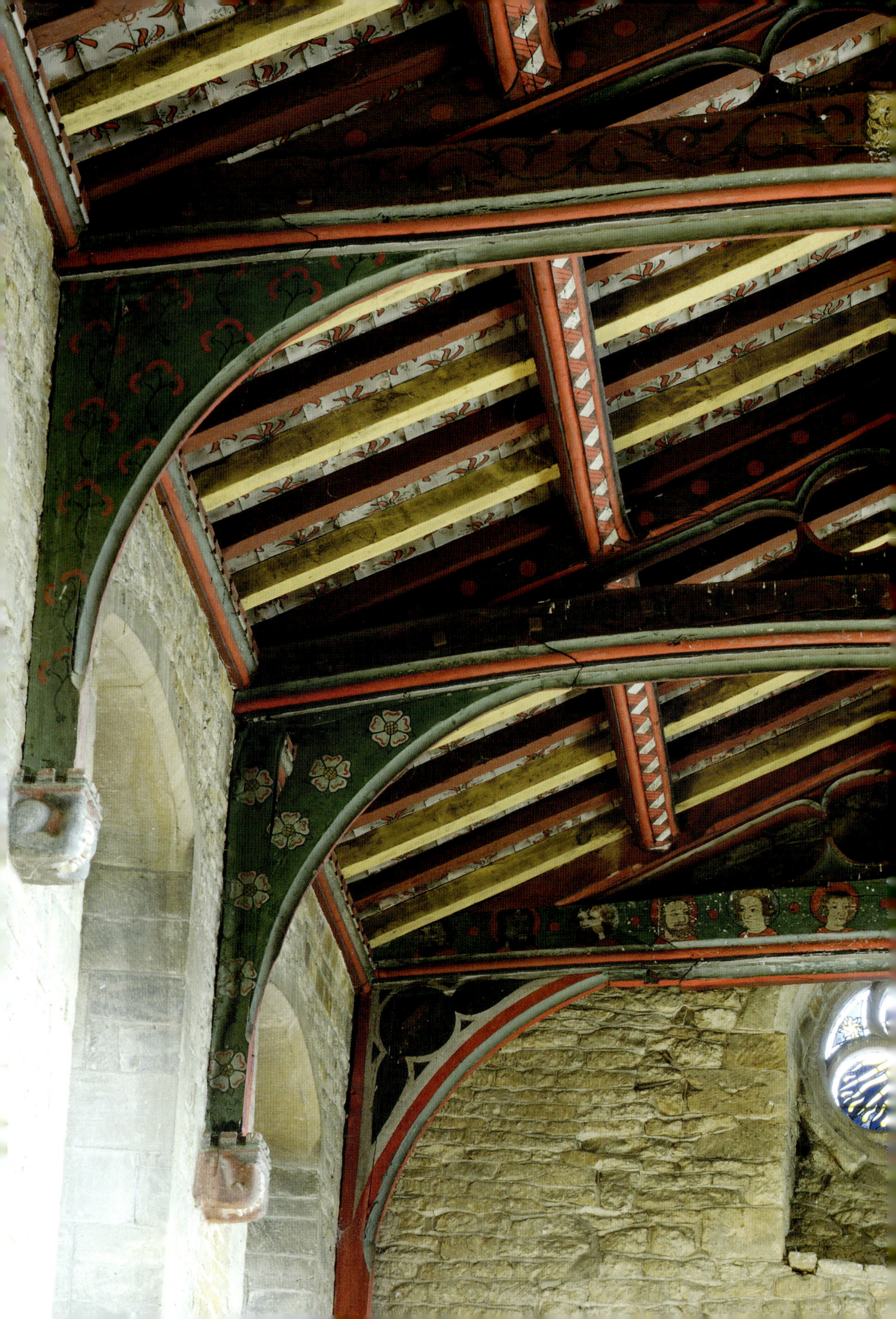

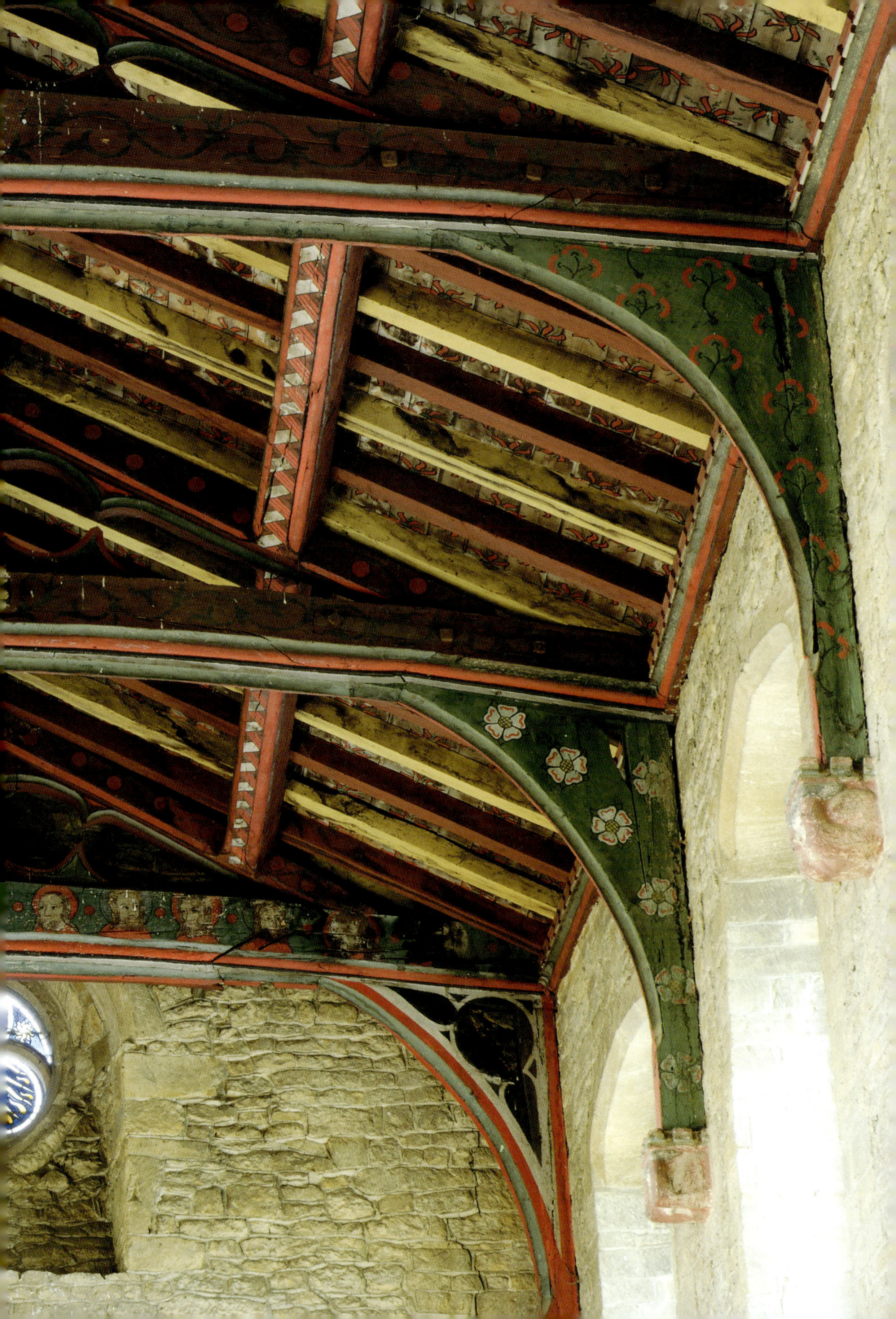

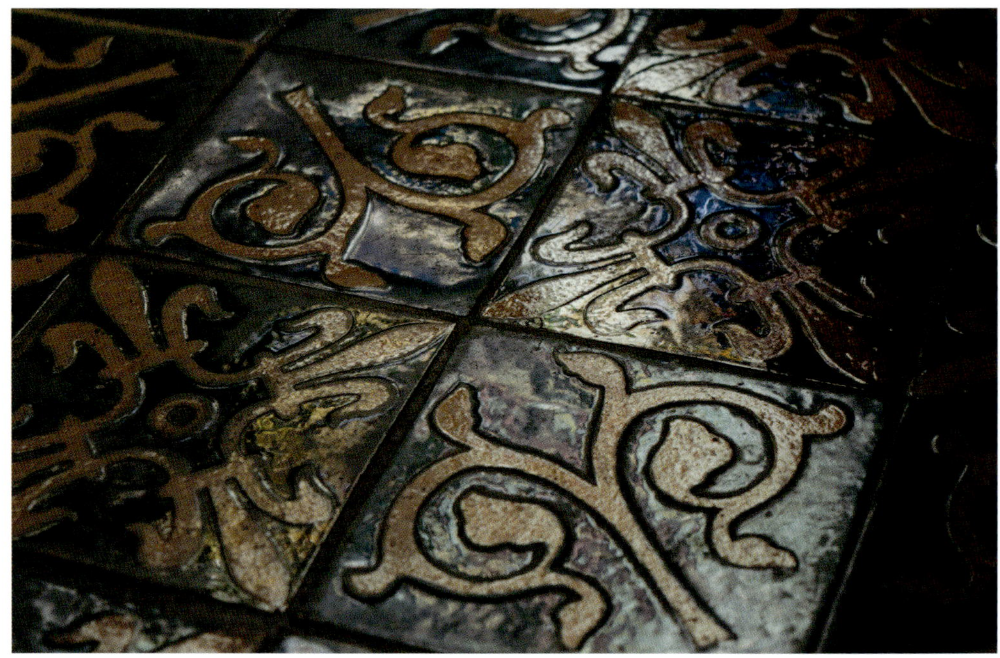

Floor tiles by William Godwin of Lugwardine, based on the original encaustic tiles

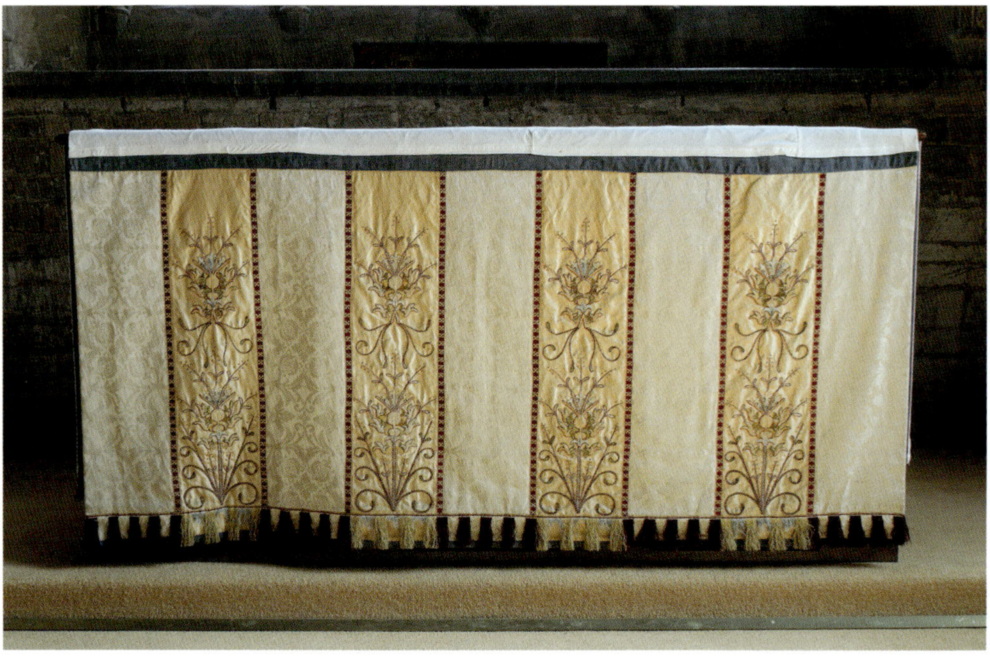

Altar frontal designed by George Gilbert Scott Jnr, and embroidered by Revd Buckley's wife and sister

At major festivals the church still makes use of the altar frontal, made of gold fabric, designed by George Gilbert Scott Junior, and embroidered by Buckley's wife and sister. It became increasingly common practice for the Scott partnership to incorporate specially-designed fabrics into their overall decorative schemes for churches. Art embroidery of this type later became one of the characteristics of the Arts and Crafts movement, and one of the design services offered by the firm of Morris & Co.

The church is not generally rich in monuments or memorials, but does possess an interesting early Jacobean-style wall monument of 1701 to John Barkesdale (the local Lord of the Manor) in the south aisle; together with hatchments (lozenge-shaped timber panels painted with coats of arms) associated with the Horton family pew, which may have been imported from London or created for the mid nineteenth-century reburial. There are two noteworthy brasses in the chancel. Beneath the carpet at the east end of the chancel is a brass commemorating Revd Ralph Churton, Rector of All Saints (1792–1831). Among other things he is remembered for his church school in the village, and for devising an indexing system that remains standard at the University of Oxford, where he was educated at Brasenose College. A further brass plaque, this one on the north wall of the chancel, commemorates Revd William Buckley who oversaw the restoration, re-ordering and reglazing of the church in the 1860s.

CHURCHYARD

Among the lichen-splashed ironstone gravestones, one monument in particular stands out. On the south-east side of the church, level with the chancel and fenced in by iron railings, is the unusual Horton Tomb, erected for her family by Mary Ann Horton in 1865. Her father, William Horton, had made his fortune from elastic stockings, enabling him to purchase a vast estate, including Middleton Cheney. It has an elaborate gothic canopy in Portland Stone, with a crocketed, polygonal roof borne on an arcade of cusped arches and marble piers. It was designed by Oxford architect William Wilkinson. Wilkinson also designed a neighbouring house (The Holt, built in 1864 but demolished in 1973), but is perhaps best known for the Randolph Hotel in Oxford. The carving of the tomb is by Thomas Earp and the wrought iron railings are by Messrs Thomasin of Birmingham. Thomas Earp (1828–93) was a popular designer of High Victorian church fixtures and fittings, and also designed the 'Eleanor Cross' at Charing Cross, London in 1863 (an interpretation of the original thirteenth-century Eleanor Crosses erected by

Edward 1), and the pulpit at St Michael and All Angels on the Hughenden Estate, Buckinghamshire in 1891. The Horton Tomb was restored in 1995 following a fundraising campaign in the village.

A site on the north side of the church, close to the First World War monument, is reputed to be the final resting place of 46 Parliamentarian soldiers who lost their lives in the English Civil War, during a battle at 'Town Field in Middleton Cheney'. They were buried here on Sunday 7 May, 1642. In all, it is recorded that 217 Parliamentarians were killed and 300 taken prisoner – along with their brass canon, 400 muskets, 150 pikes and almost 500 swords.

In the south-western segment of the churchyard is a large tomb erected in memory of the Croome and Wise families. Robert Croome was a member of the Royal College of Surgeons, and known to have used the new Smallpox vaccination in the Banbury area. In Middleton Cheney he is reputed to have been the first doctor in the United Kingdom to vaccinate all the pupils in a school. As a result there was rioting in Banbury. However the school children all survived. His son, William Frederick Croome, was also a doctor and is commemorated in the dedication for the east window.

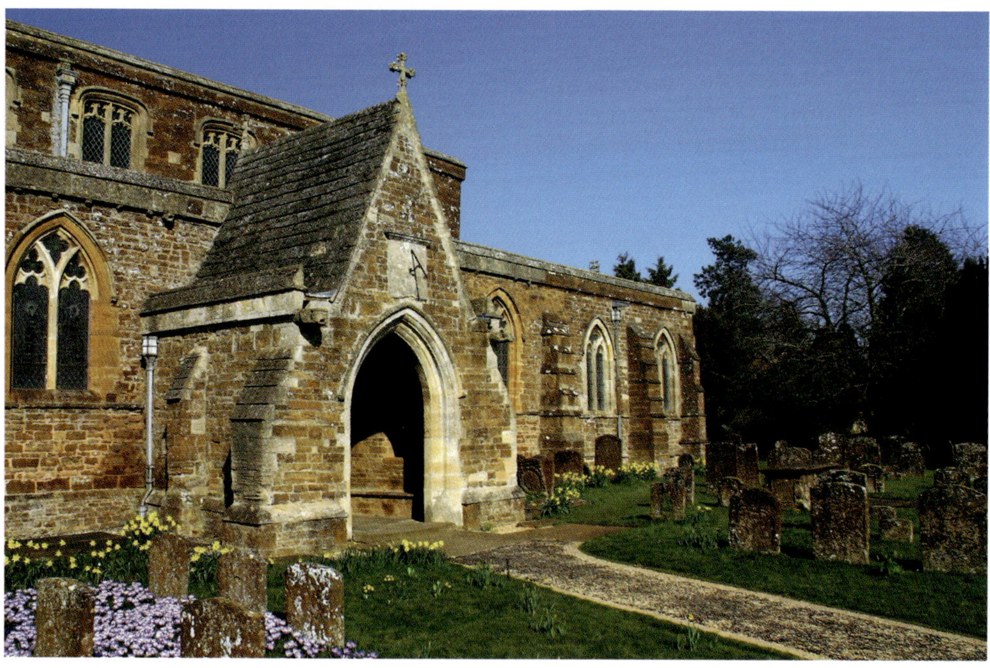

All Saints Church and churchyard looking north-east, with the south porch in the foreground
(*photograph copyright © David Thompson*)

2

Morris and the Making of Stained Glass

S TAINED glass within a church building undoubtedly helps to bring the
architecture alive. The earliest ecclesiastical examples of the use of coloured
glass in windows have been found at abbey sites in Italy and England (at Jarrow
and Monkwearmouth). As an art form, painting on glass developed in England
in the late eleventh century. Glaziers from northern France, who were invited
to England to practise their craft, were highly influential during this period in
spreading their skills. By the early thirteenth century the craft of stained glass
design and manufacture for English churches had become a significant activity,
with ten workshops spread across the country. Starting with simple patterns,
glass design was developed over time to depict single human figures, then to
narrative windows telling a story in a connected series of 'panes'. There is a good
example of this narrative treatment in All Saints, Middleton Cheney, telling the
life of Jesus through eight panes in the chancel north windows (*see pp. 16–17*).

Medieval English church stained glass suffered from periods of deliberate destruction and prolonged neglect for over a century. The process started
with the Dissolution of the Monasteries (1536–40) with specific legislation
against 'Popery' (adherence to the Pope, rather than the Church of England),
followed by neglect in the reign of Edward VI (1547–53), and destruction in
the Civil War and Puritan Commonwealth (1642–60). The destruction and
loss has continued to the present day, as a result of vandalism, neglect, lack
of funding for repairs and the decommissioning of redundant churches. A
revival in church stained glass occurred in the late eighteenth and nineteenth
centuries, the art form becoming increasingly popular during the early part
of the reign of Queen Victoria. However, it went into decline again on cost
grounds during the Long Recession of 1873–96, which particularly afflicted
Britain, Western Europe and North America.

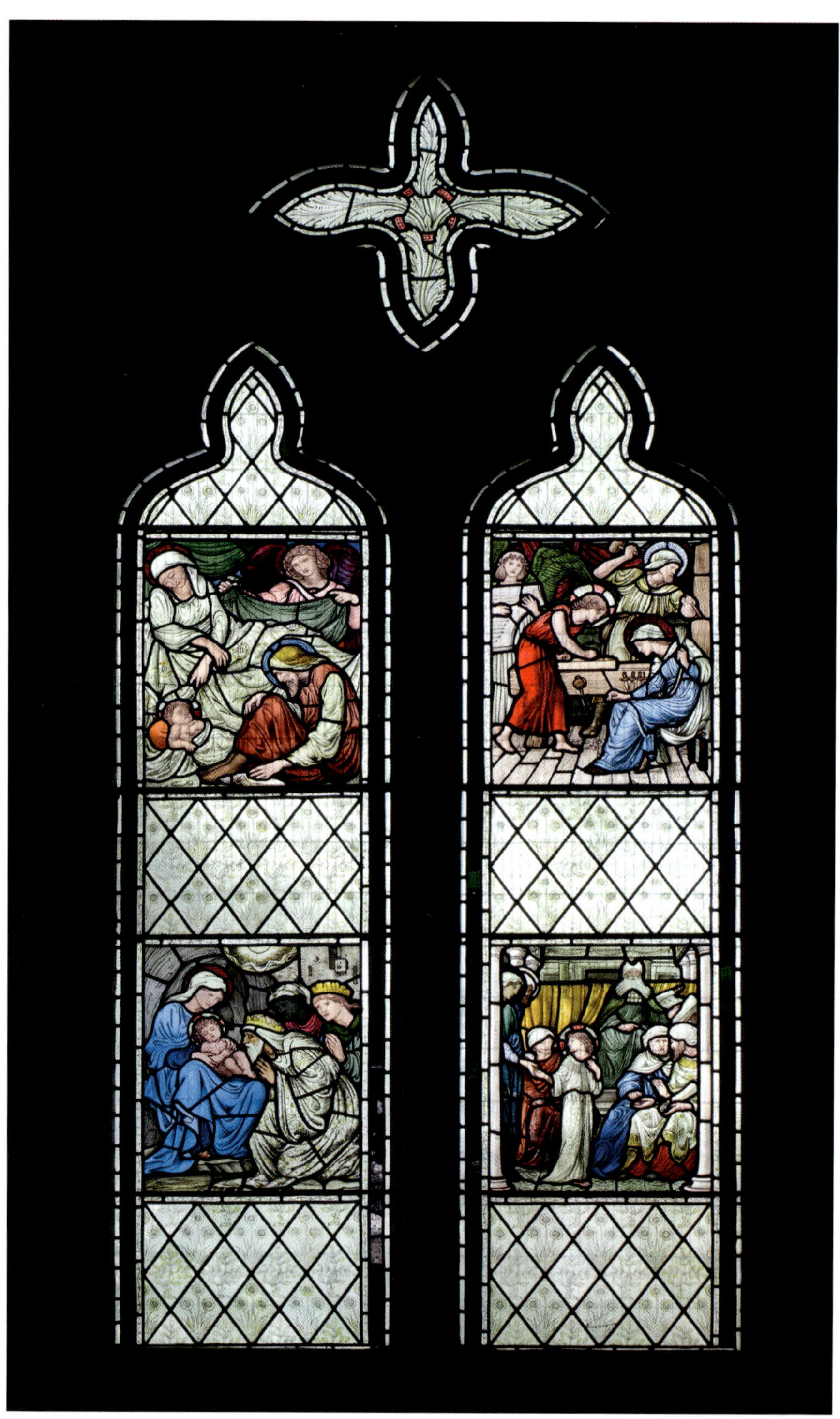

The chancel north window (west), depicting scenes from the early Life of Jesus

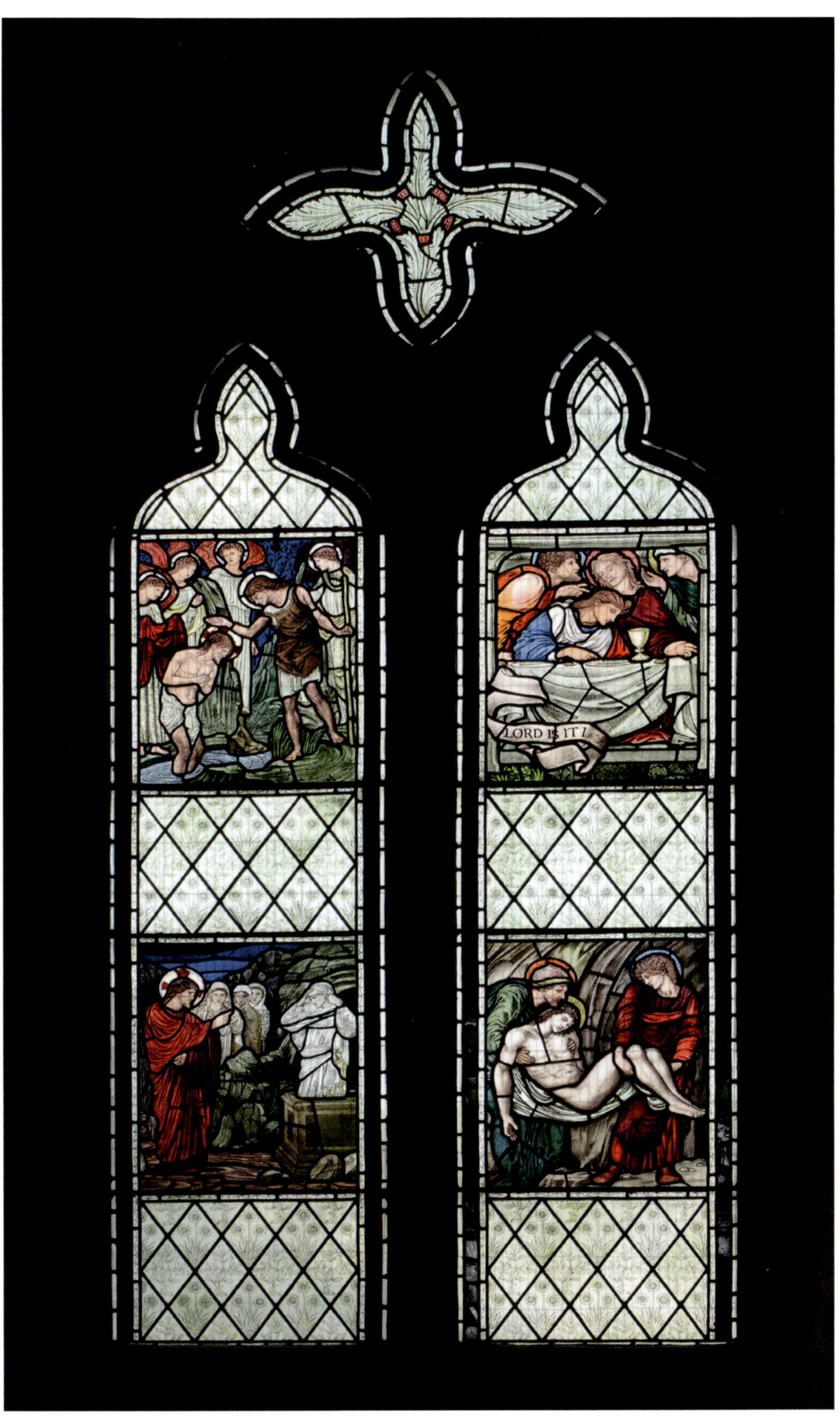

The chancel north window (east), depicting scenes from the adult Life of Jesus

The creation by William Morris of his first business in 1861 fell almost by serendipity in the middle of the early Victorian period, much to his artistic and financial advantage. There was a boom in new church-building in the Victorian era, and a large church-going community brought Pre-Raphaelite art, through stained glass windows, to a much wider audience than the display in galleries of their traditional oil painting would ever have achieved.

All Saints was a part of this wave of enthusiasm for stained glass. Aside from a medieval shard discovered in 2002, there is no clear evidence for the stained glass that may have existed prior to the church's restoration in 1865 when its east window was commissioned from Morris by Susan Croome, in memory of her doctor husband William and infant son. The east window was to become the first part of an overall scheme of glass coordinated by George Gilbert Scott, the architect, and Revd W. Buckley, the rector at that time.

Morris and Edward Burne-Jones were 'medievalists'. As students at Oxford University they had pored over illuminated manuscripts in the Ashmolean Museum. The pair made a number of visits to Europe to view medieval art, for example in the Musée de Cluny in Paris, and to northern French cathedrals, such as Chartres with its renowned, intensely-coloured stained glass windows. The exposure to these sources was a major influence upon Morris's early work. In addition, Burne-Jones also travelled with John Ruskin on a lengthy tour of Italy, where exposure to Italian art led to a significant change in his artistic style – a result of the fusion of Renaissance painting techniques with his love of medievalism. This had a major positive impact on his window design work.

Through the 1861 establishment of the firm of Morris, Marshall, Faulkner and Co., Morris himself made a significant contribution to the revival of stained glass windows in England. The aim for the firm was to resurrect the lost skills of medieval craftsmen, and to produce fine art objects of outstanding design and quality. The business model was to form a partnership of artists who would work closely with those responsible for the manufacture of the pieces. In many cases the artists would be creating the pieces from beginning to end themselves. Although Morris was very 'hands-on' himself, in reality this partnership business model was never fully realised.

The firm was awarded commissions by architects, such as G.F. Bodley, for church stained glass windows, based upon the firm's design creativity and their desire to take a fresh approach to the whole medium. One of the strengths of the firm was that the designers' combination of oil and watercolour painting with stained glass creation, often using live models, took their work into the sphere of high art. The initial problem was finding draughtsmen who could translate traditional paintings into painting for glass; however, by 1865 the business handled 20 projects in that year.

A distinguishing feature of Morris's personal contribution was his preferred use of a more natural range of colours, rather than the sharp, intense medieval colours still used by the firm's stained glass competitors. At All Saints, it is understood that approximately 70% of the glass here is Fired Painted Glass, and that some insufficient firing may account for the colour loss in parts of the west window. Ford Madox Brown shared Morris's liking for lighter colours (made possible by varying the timing of the firing of the glass), criticising earlier Pre-Raphaelite glass as 'kaleidoscopic' and 'painful'. Morris became renowned for his lighter interpretation of medieval glass, which was given the name 'New Glass' and adopted by the Arts and Crafts movement.

For the firm's early stained glass works, Morris was responsible for colour, whilst his colleague, the architect Philip Webb, was responsible for layout. Ford Madox Brown slowly became more involved. Taking his art very seriously, he produced over 90 designs, while Morris contributed 150 designs. In 1874 Madox Brown left the firm after a dispute over finances, and was replaced by the outstanding artist Edward Burne-Jones, who was appointed the principal designer of what became the most influential stained glass studio of the nineteenth century. The combination of Burne-Jones's romantic realism and Morris's versatile pattern-making proved a winning formula.

Morris had a superb sense of the use of colour, but he was not a great figurative artist in comparison with some of his colleagues, particularly his university friend Burne-Jones. Morris's main interests lay in colour, compositional details and the overall design unity of large windows. The 1865 east window at All Saints required the cooperation of five different artists, a collaboration achieved by Morris through his talents as a team leader. The subtle use of colours and their decreasing density from bottom to top, as deployed by Morris in this window, illustrate his artistic vision at the age of only thirty.

Of particular importance to Morris was impact through the representation of the window's figures in three dimensions. A particular device he employed was to allow a figure to break into the window's surrounding border. This creates a sense of movement, and there are some highly effective examples of the garments of figures doing this in the east widow at All Saints. In a panel by Morris, featuring Eve and St Mary, he creates a sense of procession by having the hand of Eve and the lily carried by St Mary breaking into the frame of the image.

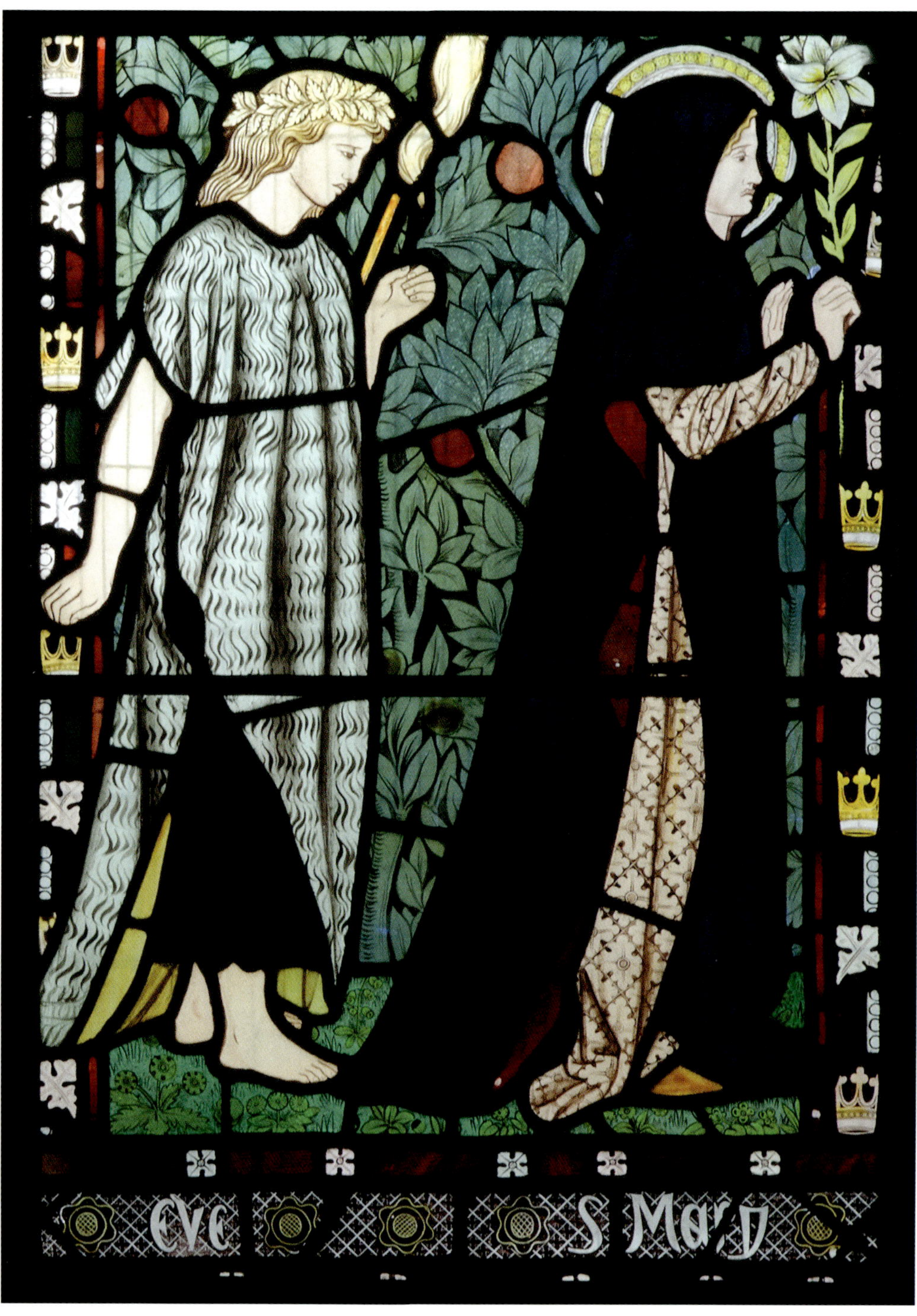

The figures of Eve and St Mary in one of the panels of the east window, their hands breaking the frame and suggesting movement (see *also the cartoon frontispiece opposite the title page*)

Morris was arguably less accomplished as an artist than many of his colleagues, and this panel is also a good example of his trying to mitigate his difficulties in drawing figures and their clothing by depicting figures in semi-profile.

Morris also had an interest in plant shapes and botany. In 1865 he began to introduce these forms into stained glass backgrounds in order to fill in the gaps between figures two-dimensionally, choosing designs loosely related to the context of the figure. Prior to this, symmetrical, small and repeated light-coloured patterns, called 'diapers', had been the traditional backgrounds in stained glass. Morris discovered how to treat the surface of blue glass to create a range of greens, essential for producing images of plant material. The east window at All Saints has a number of background plant motifs by Morris, such as leaves and splitting ripe fruit, used in his wallpaper and tile designs at around the same time. In the creation of a window panel, the drawing of the figure and its background were thus often two separate processes, carried out by two different artists.

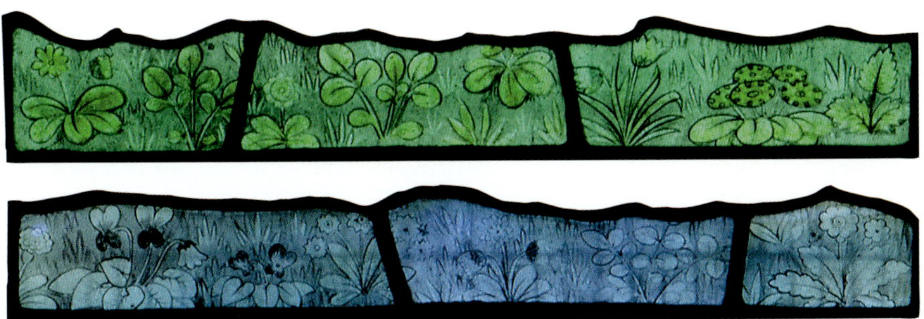
Details of the floral backgrounds in the Twelve Tribes of Israel panels in the east window

Morris possessed great energy and a restless manner, but also got involved in too many things at once. He had a reputation for being disorganised with respect to office processes, such as customer orders and accounts. In 1868 Henry James described him as 'an extraordinary example of a delicate sensitive genius and taste'. Morris was, however, good at talent-spotting, and at matching a person's skills to the job, and he was not averse to poaching talent from rival firms. He was also a very practical man. His experiments in adding silver salts to glass to produce a range of yellows became a feature of his best late-1860s' windows; yellows helping to make the interior of a church light and bright. The east window at All Saints has some good examples of his use of yellows as accent points.

The amount of effort that went into design and manufacture, together with the high salaries which the partners paid themselves (Morris surreptitiously spent a lot of money on books and wine), meant that the prices charged by the firm were high and their customer-base for ecclesiastical stained glass limited to the well-to-do. The designers were paid according to their skills and reputation. For example, Dante Gabriel Rossetti and Edward Burne-Jones commanded higher fees for their window design than Morris. Initially, the designs were anonymous, but Morris saw the marketing value in reputation, such that when the firm's 1862 catalogue was printed it contained the statement: 'Mr Burne-Jones entrusts us alone with the execution of his stained glass'.

Although the creation of stained glass by Morris & Co. for churches was a serious business, the members of the firm were not averse to playing practical jokes on one another at business meetings. This developed into Rossetti, Morris and Burne-Jones introducing pictures of one another into their windows, with Morris being allocated teasing appearances as 'underdog' figures by the other two. In the east window this practice is transformed (with Morris in charge) into Morris appearing as St Peter, Burne-Jones as St Paul, Jane (Morris's wife) as St Mary Magdalene, and Georgiana, Burne-Jones's wife, as St Agnes. Ford Madox Brown also added his own self portrait as St John. Morris developed a habit of putting himself into his works, to the extent that this became a common criticism of him.

Morris was aided in the rediscovery of medieval techniques of glass manufacture and its subsequent advancement as an artistic medium in the 1800s by progression in the science of chemistry. A number of people had worked on the technicalities of recreating medieval glass, with its brilliancy and transparency, before Morris entered the world of stained glass. Central to this was the pioneering work at Whitefriars Glass of London, run by James Powell and his three sons. This was not only England's longest running glass company (c.1680–1981) but also one of the most productive and inventive, becoming a world leader in its field. Initially the company made only decanters and wine glasses, but in 1854 they started experimenting with chemical mixes to achieve medieval-looking coloured glass for church window restoration projects.

While Powell and Sons manufactured stained glass windows under their own name, they also provided glass to other stained glass firms, including Morris & Co. Powell and Sons subsequently supplied Burne-Jones with wholesale glass with the right mix of bubbles and natural colours to match medieval glass for his projects. When Harry James Powell, the grandson of James Powell, joined

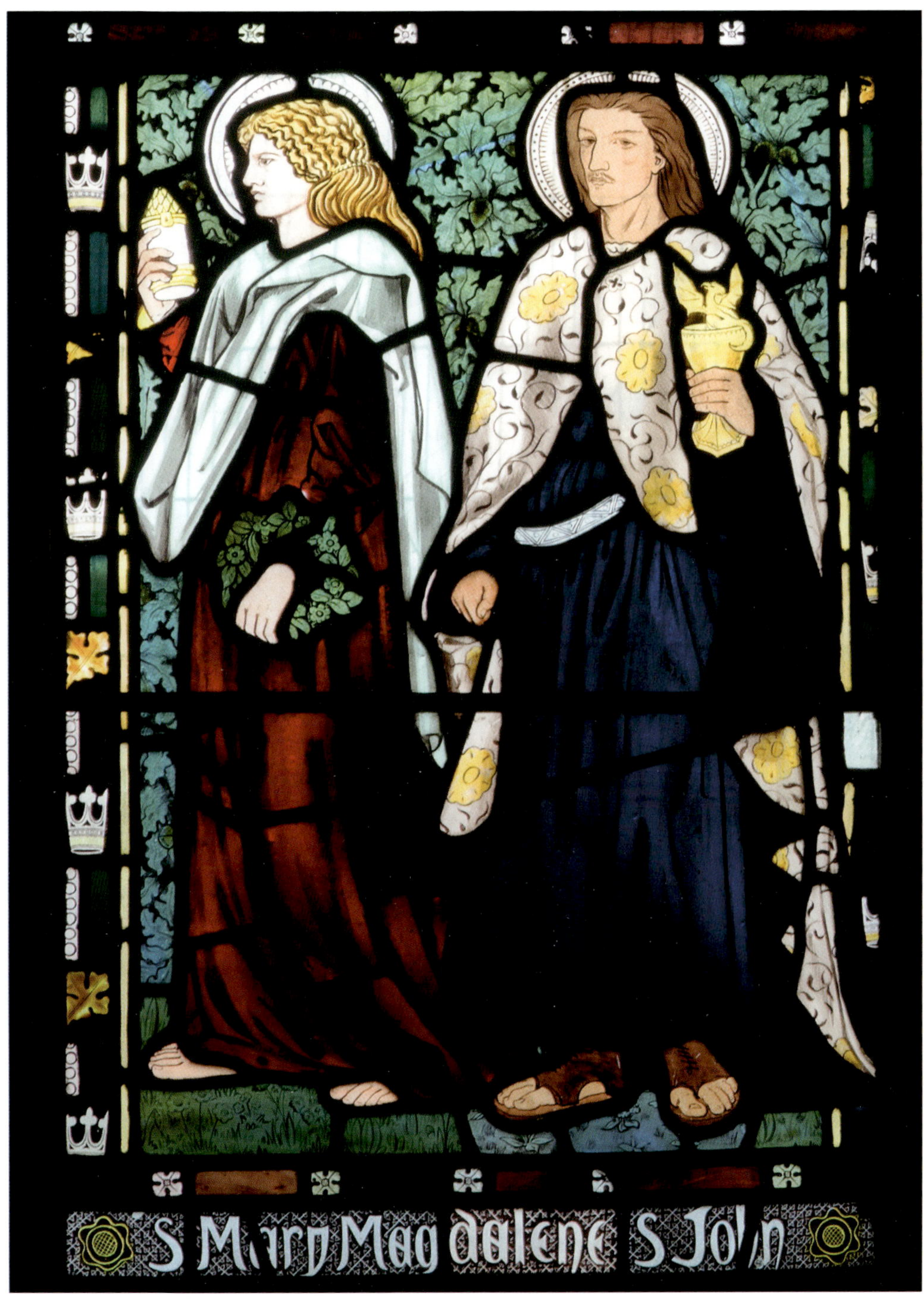

The figures of St Mary Magdalene and St John in the east window (the figure of St Mary is believed to have been modelled on Morris's wife, Jane)

the firm on graduating from Oxford in 1875, his scientific training helped to propel innovation in glass technology at Whitefriars and contributed to establishing its international reputation, with Morris's firm becoming a significant long-term customer, buying only the best of their subtly-coloured glass.

With his broad range of interests it was inevitable that Morris would move on to do other things, his most active period of personal engagement with stained glass being limited to the period 1862–69. The late 1860s saw a slump in orders for ecclesiastical glass due to the economic instability preceding the Long Depression. Morris then led a diversification of his business into textiles and wallpapers, creating a whole interior design style and a brand still widely recognised today. Stained glass remained in the firm's portfolio, with commissions mainly supervised by Burne-Jones. Morris died in 1898. The firm, however, continued up until 1940.

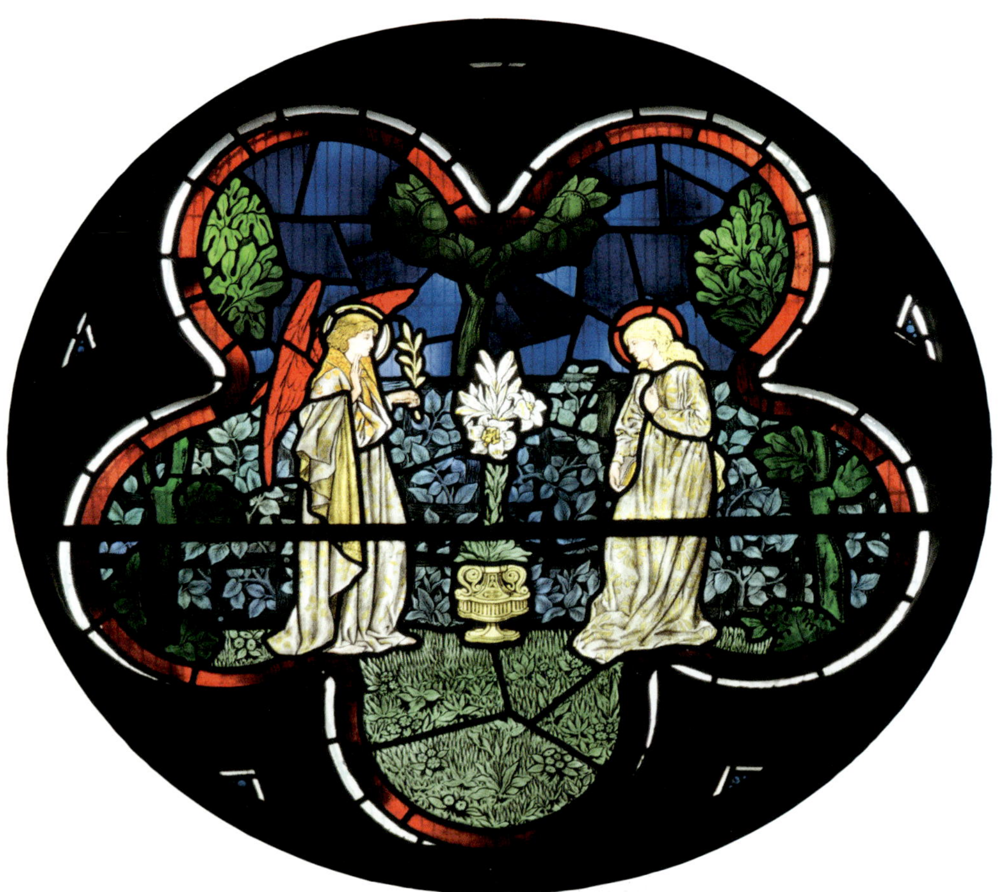

The Annunciation light in the top of the north aisle east window

3

The Morris & Co. Stained Glass Windows

THE Morris & Co. windows that are the main focus of visitor attention at All Saints were installed between 1865 and 1893. While it is almost certain that the windows in the church would have contained coloured glass at some point prior to the restoration in the 1860s, we have very little evidence for the glass that may have existed before 1864.

As part of the extensive restoration of the church carried out by architects George Gilbert Scott and his son, Gilbert Scott Junior, the tracery in most of the windows was renewed, reportedly in its original form. The renewed east window was in place for the 1865 reopening, and it is likely that the design and construction of the tracery by Scott and Scott Junior went hand-in-hand with the design of the glass coordinated and directed by William Morris, with Revd Buckley contributing to the ongoing design. This may also be true of the south east chancel window, dedicated to Archdeacon Churton, Rector at Middleton Cheney (1792–1831), as correspondence with Brasenose suggests that Buckley was hoping to have this completed by the reopening (though this was completed later, and dedicated in 1871).

All Saints Church:
Stained glass in order of installation

1)	East window	1865
2)	North aisle north window	1866–67
3)	North aisle east window	1866–67
4)	Chancel south window	1868–70
5)	West window	1871
6)	Gable window	1871
7)	South aisle east window	1885
8)	South aisle west window	1891
9)	Chancel north window (w)	1893
10)	Chancel north window (e)	1893

In order to gain a sense of the development of styles in the windows as they were installed in All Saints Church from 1865 to 1893 by the firm of Morris & Co., the following details are provided in order of installation. It should be noted, however, that certain designs may long predate installation. The chronological account seeks, where possible, to identify the individual artists responsible for the windows, and to give further information on each commission and the subject-matter in each case (see also the church plan opposite p. 1).

1)   THE EAST WINDOW (*1865*)

The east window – appropriately known as the 'All Saints' window – was the first window from the firm of Morris, Marshall, Faulkner and Co. to be installed in All Saints Church, with the majority of the individual designs dating from 1864. The east window was dedicated to the Croome family. William Croome (son of Robert Croome) was a physician who died in 1862 at the age of just 31, having lived in Middleton Cheney and then Banbury. The brass dedication plaque for the window is inscribed:

> To the Glory of God. SUSAN CROOME in memory of her husband
> WILLIAM FREDERICK CROOME and their infant son 1865.

The east window represents a major production of the firm, with the panels of Adam and Noah, and St Agnes and St Alban, included in the firm's display at the 1864 Exhibition of Stained Glass at South Kensington. Overall, the window has been described as, 'a triumphant success, a masterpiece and one of the most splendid achievements in all English stained glass.' (*Sewter, 1974*); and of exhibiting, 'brilliant depths of colour and the dynamic, fluid compositions … unparalleled in Victorian stained glass' (*Barringer, Rosenfeld & Smith, 2012*).

Of particular note is the overall coherence of the design, achieved despite the fact that all but one of the partners in the firm had a hand in its making. Such design coherence was a characteristic of the firm's work from an early date, with an even earlier window ('King Rene's Honeymoon' of *c*.1863, now in the V&A) displaying similar characteristics.

Although Philip Webb generally had overall responsibility for stained glass design at the firm up until 1869, it appears that the guiding hand for the

OPPOSITE: The east window

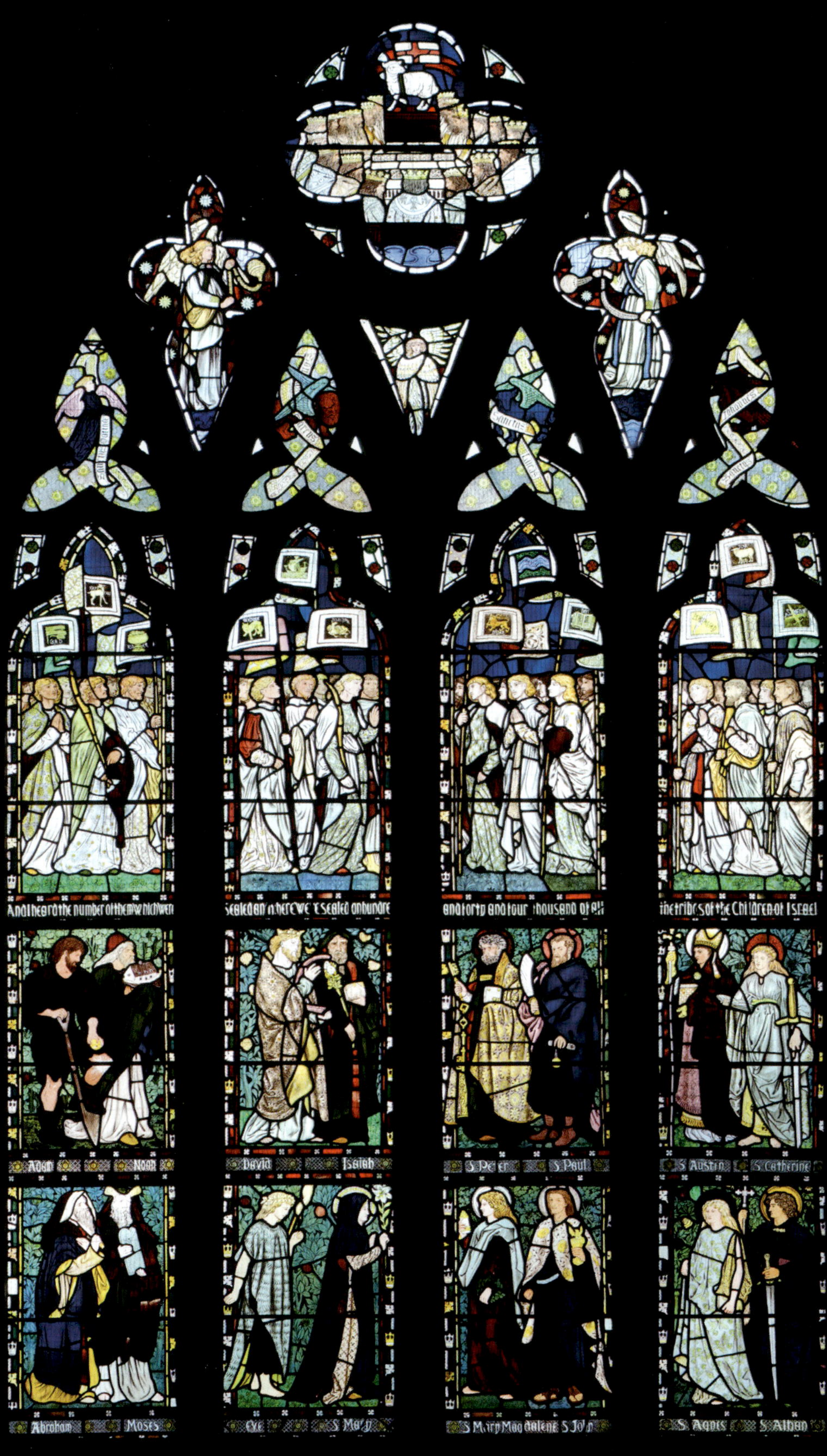

And he read the number of them which were
sealed and there were sealed an hundred
and forty and four thousand of all
the tribes of the Children of Israel
Adam   Noah   David   Isaiah   S Peter   S Paul   S Austin   S Catherine
Abraham   Moses   Eve   S Mary   S Mary Magdalene S John   S Agnes   S Alban

east window at Middleton Cheney may have belonged to Morris. We know little of the creative process for this complex window, but it has been noted that, 'the most successful windows, such as the east window at Middleton Cheney, doubtless resulted from an intimate collaboration between client and artists, in which the contribution of the client, especially in regard to subject-matter, may well have been of vital importance.' (*Sewter, 1974*). Whilst Webb's may not have been the guiding hand here, his contributions to the east window, including to the backgrounds he designed along with Morris, are regarded as some of his best work.

In terms of its overall structure, the east window is composed of a series of illustrated tiers jostling with figures, many in motion, carrying symbolic items, looking inwards symmetrically across the design, thus drawing the eye in and up towards the top panel – the Adoration of the Lamb. The figures comprise Saints, early Christian martyrs and the Twelve Tribes of Israel. The upper panels are structured around the Epistle for All Saints' Day (Revelation 7:2–12) and the Epistle for Trinity Sunday (Revelation 4:1–11).

Three Old Testament sections – the figures of the Twelve Tribes of Israel, David and Isaiah, and Abraham and Moses – were designed by the Jewish artist Simeon Solomon (1840–1905). He was evidently much admired by his fellow artists, with Edward Burne-Jones quoted as saying, 'You know, Simeon, we are mere schoolboys compared with you.'

Solomon was only 25 years of age when he designed these windows (his first window designs) having had his first exhibition in London two years before. Solomon's designs at Middleton Cheney were later reused by Morris – albeit incorporating variations of colour and background – in North Church, Greenock (also known as Old West Kirk before its stone-by-stone move to Greenock's central Esplanade in 1925–28 to allow for dockyard development, and now known as Lyle Kirk.) Solomon's images at Middleton Cheney suggest his early interest in the Old Testament, with his Jewish heritage perhaps giving a clue as to the allocation of his contribution subject-matter (his 'Moses' was exhibited at the Royal Academy in 1860). The homoeroticism of the 'Tribes', meanwhile, marks his move to Aestheticism.

Solomon produced a large body of work and exhibited, despite a chaotic lifestyle which led to reputational damage and meant that he lived for much of the time in poverty until his death at the St Giles Workhouse at Bloomsbury in 1905. Recent years have witnessed a rapid growth in Solomon scholarship and appreciation.

ADORATION OF THE LAMB (*by Edward Burne-Jones, 1863–64, originally for St Edmund Hall, Oxford*)

The Lamb symbolises Christ as the victorious *Agnus Dei* (1 Corinthians 5:7 and Revelation 5:13) carrying a banner, in this case an English pennant of victory and with a gash in its side symbolising the Crucifixion. The Lamb of God is depicted on a red altar surrounded by a circle of 24 crowned Elders (Revelation 5:8). It is worth noting that each of the kings illustrated here wears a different cloak and crown, symbolising universal acknowledgement.

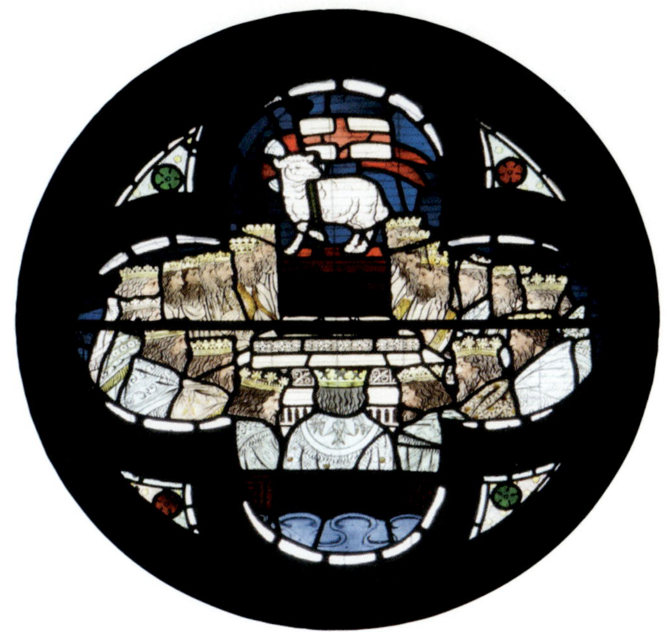

The Adoration of the Lamb, from the top of the east window

ANGELS SWINGING CENSERS (*by Philip Webb*)
SERAPH WITH FOLDED WINGS (*by Edward Burne-Jones or William Morris*)
SYMBOLS OF THE FOUR EVANGELISTS (*by Philip Webb*)

The strongly-coloured figures are (*from left to right*): Matthew (as a winged man or angel), Mark (as a winged lion), Luke (as a winged ox or bull) and John (as an eagle). Each figure is loosely entwined with a fluttering ribbon or scroll carrying his name, against a fabric-like background dotted with yellow roses.

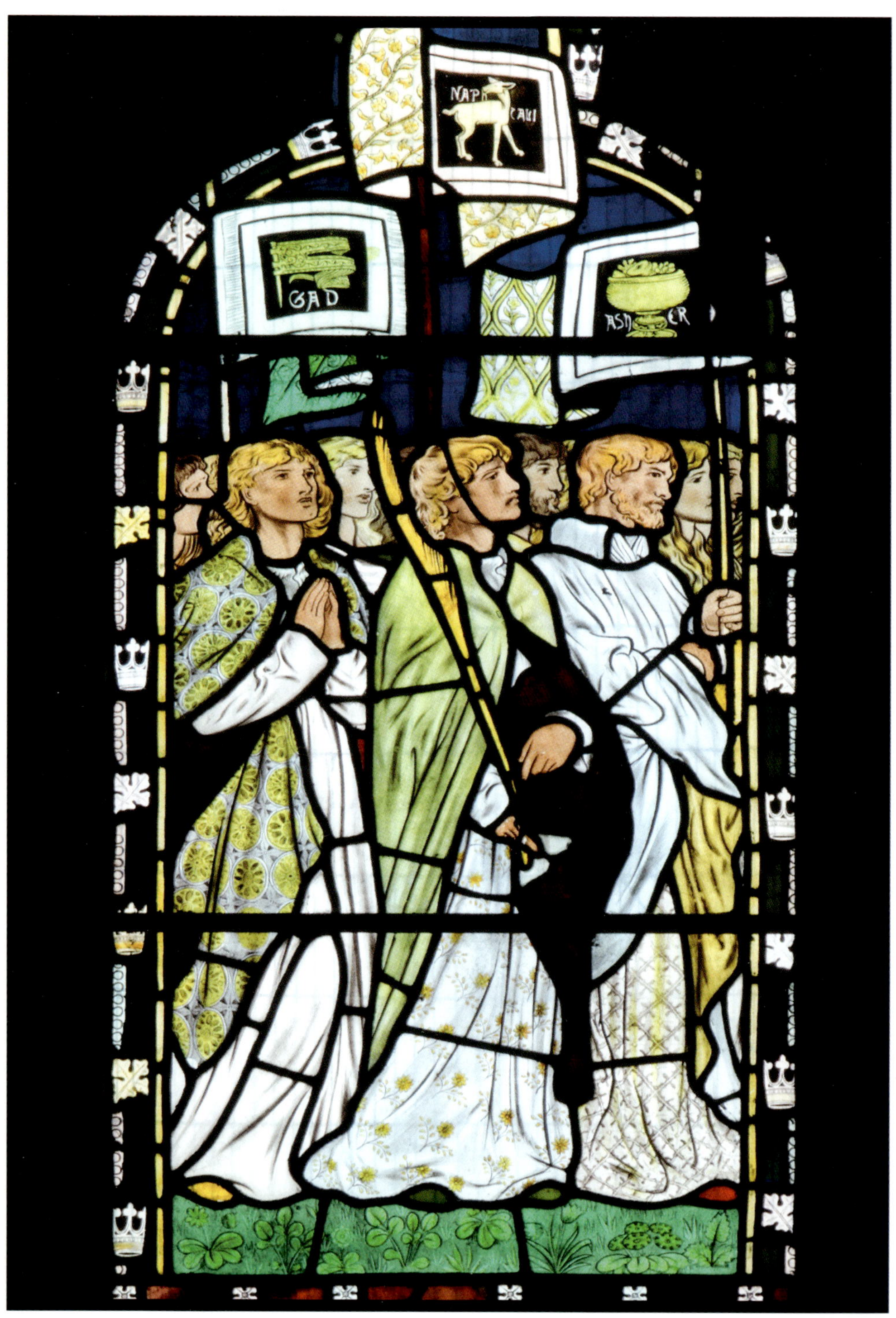

The Twelve Tribes of Israel (*detail*) by Simeon Solomon, from the east window

THE TWELVE TRIBES OF ISRAEL (*figures by Simeon Solomon and emblems with tribal names by Philip Webb, 1864, the designs originally for embroidery*)

The Twelve Tribes, descended from the sons of Jacob, are identified by the named flags (three flags in each of the four lights). The procession of Saints and Martyrs/ the Twelve Tribes of Israel in this window is a depiction unique to Middleton Cheney. The four lights are crowded with figures processing towards the centre of the window, with eyes gazing upwards, lightly clad in white robes with details in reds, yellow and pale green. Movement is suggested not only by the animated poses of the figures and the rippling folds of the robes, but also by the figures breaking into the frames, as if they were passing behind the window and its tracery. This device gives the figures a three-dimensional effect, a technique also used elsewhere in the window.

The figures themselves are by Simeon Solomon, and are dominated by handsome and elegant men typical of the artist's work. Beneath the figures, running the full width of the window, is a text from Revelation 7:4: 'And I heard the number of them which were sealed: and there were sealed an hundred and forty and four thousand of all the tribes of the Children of Israel'. Stylistically, the figures bear comparison with those of another of the Pre-Raphaelites, Dante Gabriel Rossetti.

ADAM AND NOAH (*both figures by Ford Madox Brown, 1864. The design of Adam also appears in a window for North Church, Greenock, of 1865; that of Noah, Madox Brown's most frequently reproduced figure, in 12 other locations*)

Adam is depicted digging in the Garden of Eden, holding a golden apple in his left hand, against a background that includes both green and dark red apples. Noah is clearly identified by the Ark he carries.

DAVID AND ISAIAH (*both figures by Simeon Solomon, 1864, and both also appearing in windows for North Church, Greenock, 1865*)

The youthful King David, in a fine embroidered robe (or cope) is shown playing his harp. The Prophet Isaiah, meanwhile, stares fixedly out at the viewer, carrying his book and a rod topped with fruit and leaves (Isaiah 11:1: 'a shoot shall come up from the stem of Jesse; from his roots a branch shall bear fruit').

The background here is dotted with yellow pomegranates. The pomegranate, as well as being a symbol traditionally woven into the hems of vestments, is also one of the symbols of King Solomon. For this reason it might be tempting

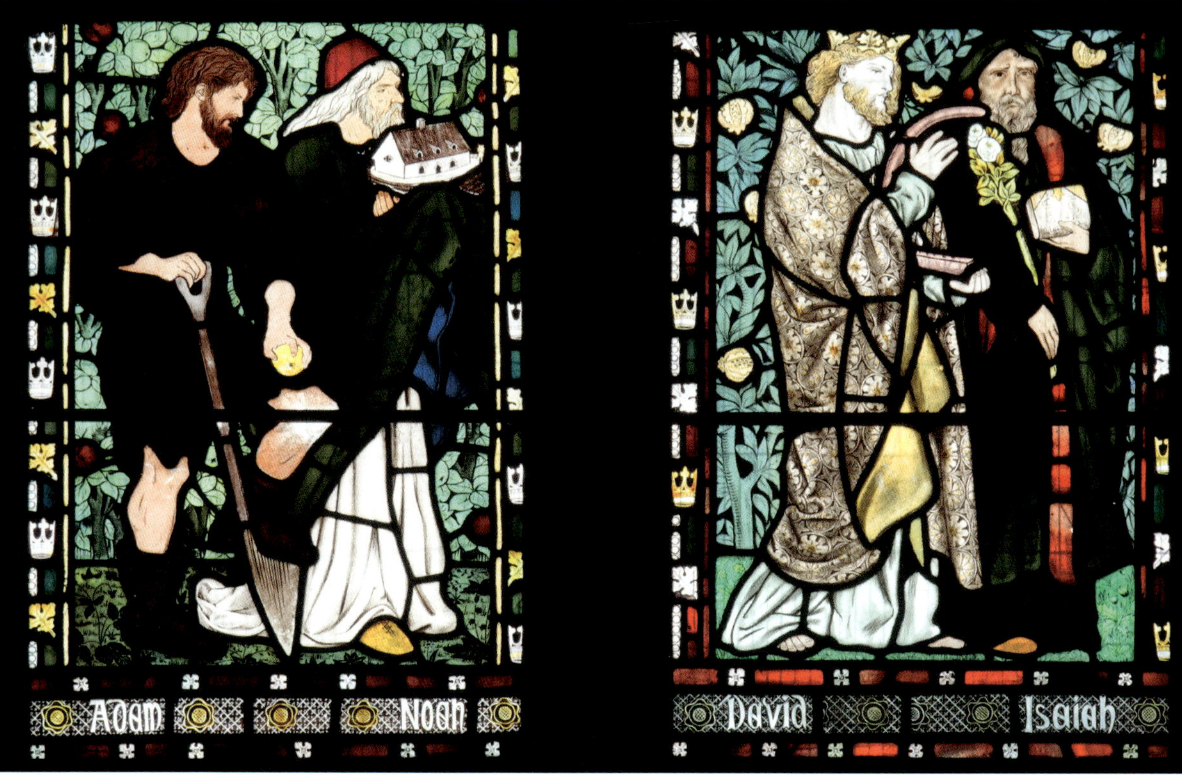

The figures of Adam and Noah (*left*), and David and Isaiah (*right*) from the east window

to speculate that the inclusion of the fruit here is a nod towards the King's artist namesake, Simeon Solomon, who was responsible for the design; however, pomegranates also appear in the background of the St Agnes and St Alban panel below, which is by Morris. Pomegranates also became a feature of some of Morris's wallpaper designs at around this time.

ST PETER AND ST PAUL (*St Peter by William Morris, 1864. The first appearance of this design, his most frequently repeated figure design, which appears in 16 other locations. St Paul by Ford Madox Brown, 1865. The design, with different colour combinations, first appearing in Bradford Cathedral in 1863, and also found in five other locations*)

The figure of St Peter is possibly a Morris self-portrait, following the traditional iconography of a saint with white tousled hair and a beard, wearing a robe covered by a gold cope. He is depicted carrying two large keys (to Heaven's Gates) together with a book representing the Gospel. Another possible self-portrait

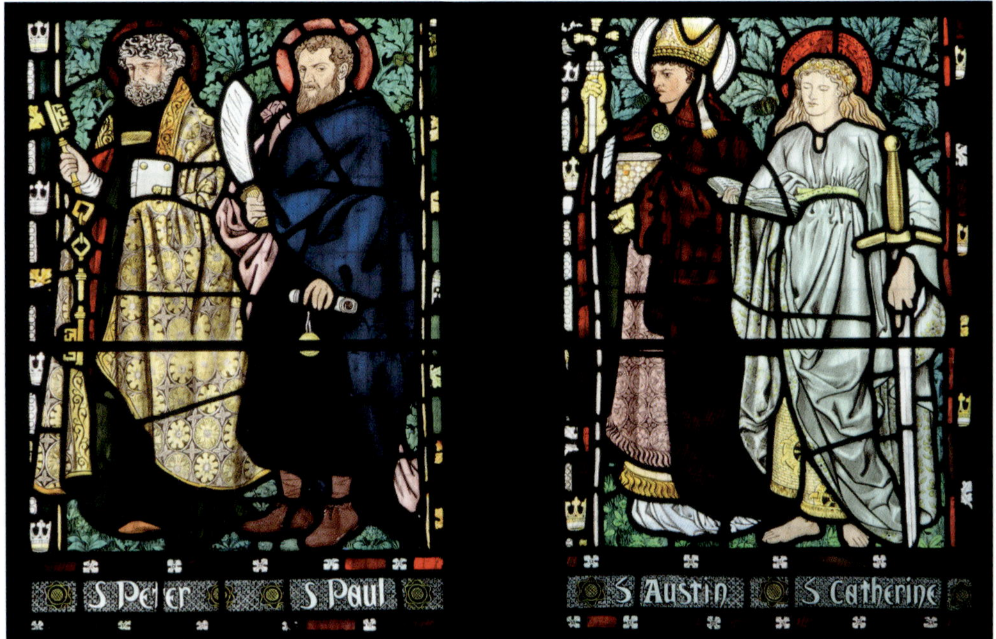

The figures of St Peter and St Paul (*left*), and St Austin and St Catherine (*right*) from the east window

in glass by Morris, of a similar date (this one with Morris as St Matthew, and perhaps more convincing) can be found in the Lady Chapel of Christ Church Cathedral in Oxford.

The figure of St Paul, wrapped in a cloak of deep blue, carries a rolled and sealed document; but also a large, flat-bladed knife or sword – the weapon by which, according to tradition, the Saint died.

ST AUSTIN AND ST CATHERINE (*both figures by William Morris, 1865. The design for St Austin appears at Bloxham, of 1868, and at six other locations. St Catherine appears in nine other locations, including All Saints in Cambridge*)

Although not certain, it seems most likely that the St Augustine referenced here is St Augustine of Canterbury (who died in 604). He was a Benedictine monk who became the first Archbishop of Canterbury in 597, and was founder of the Catholic Church in England, and therefore of the Church of England. The other possibility is St Augustine of Hippo (354–430). He was a Roman African convert whose writings continue to provide a fundamental reference for Christian teaching.

The St Austin figure in the east window has both a bishop's staff and mitre, and there is no further evidence as to his identity. However, St Augustine of Hippo's ethnic identity had been featured in earlier images, and might be expected in this window if this was the intended subject. The further inclusion of St Alban below suggests an emphasis on English Saints, which feature prominently in the window, so St Augustine of Canterbury, widely known as St Austin, seems most likely.

The figure of St Catherine is shown with a book and substantial sword, her identity confirmed by the two wheels (hence 'Catherine Wheels') visible on her yellow under-dress. St Catherine of Alexandria, to give her full title, was martyred in the fourth century, and is an enigmatic figure. Condemned as a Christian, she was to be broken on a wheel, but it was the wheel that broke and she had to be executed with a sword. The St Catherine figure is said to have been modelled on 'Janey' – the wife of William Morris. The use of family members as models was common practice, as was the use of depictions of the artists and friends in the Morris circle.

ABRAHAM AND MOSES (*both by Simeon Solomon, 1864. Both designs also appear in windows for North Church, Greenock, 1865*)

The elderly Abraham is shown holding aloft the knife with which he was willing to kill his son, Isaac, at God's command. His left hand goes to his throat and his brow is furrowed, as he appears to foresee what he must do (in the end he was redirected by God to sacrifice a sheep instead).

Next to him stands the facially similar figure of Moses, shown as the lawgiver, holding in both hands the stone tablet given to him by God on Mount Sinai, and upon which are set out the Ten Commandments.

The two forms coming out of the head of Moses are probably intended to be rays of light, though could also be interpreted as horns. In what is now generally accepted as a mistranslation by Jerome of the relevant passage in Exodus (34:29, 30 and 35) the Hebrew word '*qāran*' was said to mean 'horn' (leading to some depictions of Moses – including by the likes of Michelangelo and, later, Gustave Doré – showing him with horns). The passage in Exodus relates to Moses' return to the people after receiving the Commandments for the second time, when his face is said to have shone following his conversation with God. The translation of the Hebrew word is now generally accepted as 'emitting rays' or 'shining', and it is this interpretation that is probably represented in the east window at Middleton Cheney.

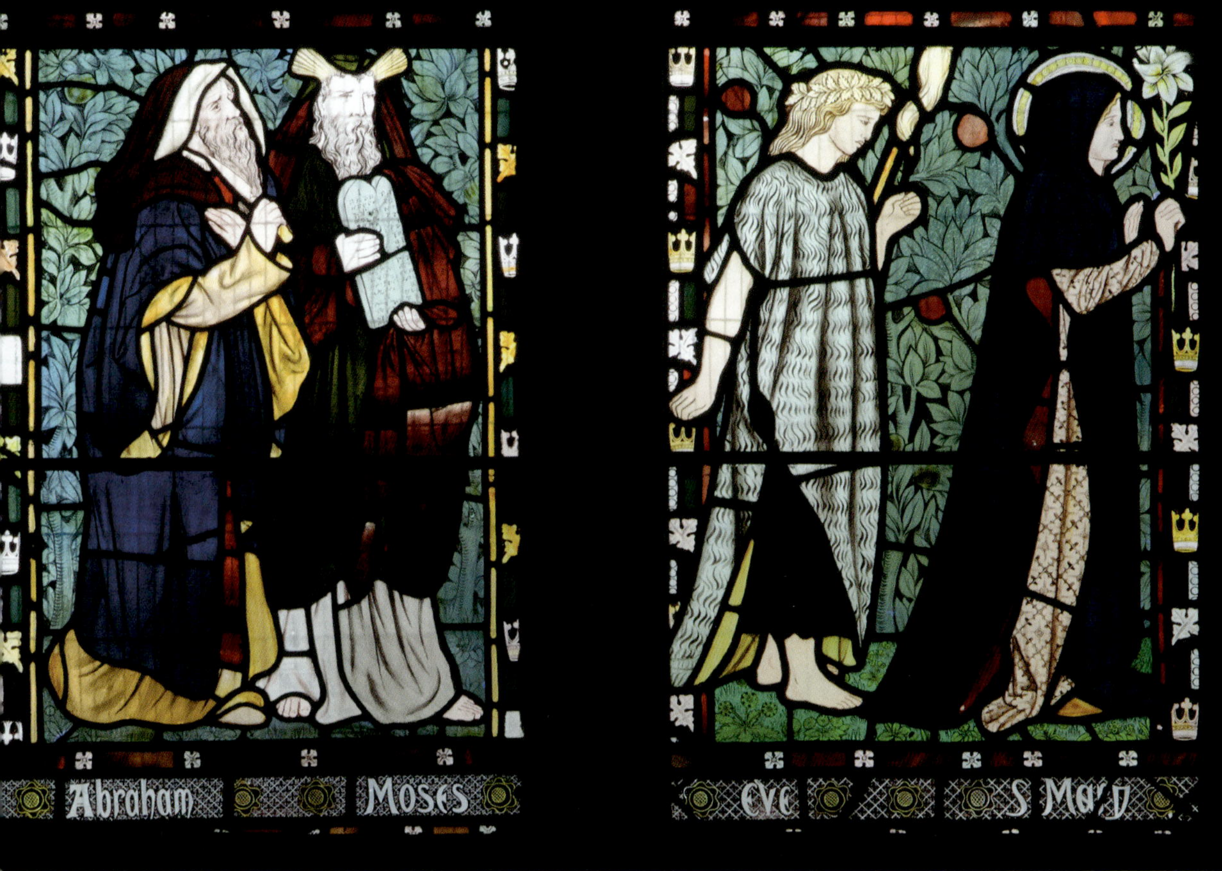

The figures of Abraham and Moses (*left*), and Eve and St Mary (*right*) from the east window

EVE AND THE VIRGIN MARY (*both by William Morris, 1864. Both designs also appear in windows for North Church, Greenock, 1865*)

Eve is shown here after the Fall, head bowed, in a pale grey-green costume, against a background dotted with the same dark red apples as those found in the Adam panel above. Eve appears to be wearing a woollen dress or cloak, and visible next to her head is a distaff (a stick onto which wool is wound for spinning). The cartoon for this figure (in the William Morris Gallery in London, and including the figure of the Virgin Mary – *see the frontispiece opposite the title page*) shows Eve spinning from a distaff.

The Virgin Mary walks before Eve, clad in her traditional blue mantle or cloak, and carrying a white lily, a symbol of virginity and purity.

ST MARY MAGDALENE AND ST JOHN (*St Mary by William Morris, 1863, also found at St Ladoca's Church at Ladock, Truro, and at Greenock, 1865. St John by Ford Madox Brown, 1863, used at Bradford Cathedral and several other locations*)

The several strands of Mary's interpreted life are drawn together in this image (*see p. 23*). The alabaster jar of ointment in her right hand, her most frequent symbol, refers to her anointing of Christ's feet (John 12:3) which she then dried with her hair. The wreath may be a reference to her being the first to observe the empty tomb at the Resurrection. It may also be intended as an Advent Wreath, symbolising God's infinite love, and usually shown as being made up of evergreen leaves to denote the hope of eternal life brought by Christ.

St John the Apostle, the Evangelist and author of Revelation, is shown (like the figures of Isaiah and St Paul above) looking out at the viewer. In his left hand he holds aloft a chalice from which, it is believed, he drank poison to prove his faith. The chalice is sometimes depicted topped with threatening serpents; however, here a small eagle is shown, the traditional symbol of the Evangelist, and a reference to the power and spread of his writings.

Medieval lettering found in the Morris windows
In many of the Morris windows in All Saints Church, we see examples of typefaces reflecting medieval designs. In all, seven typefaces can be located. None of these were found recorded in the St Bride Library in London (primarily devoted to printing, book arts, typography and graphic design). It appears that Morris wanted to try out designs with a medieval appearance. Later, while working with the Kelmscott Press, and influenced by medieval illuminated manuscripts, Morris went on to publish beautiful editions of over 50 books using typography of the highest quality.

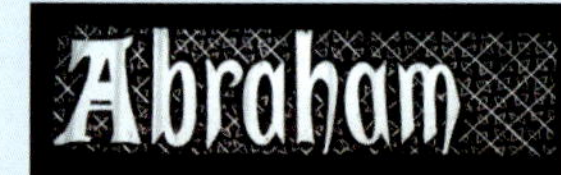

ST AGNES AND ST ALBAN (*both by William Morris, 1864, and only found at Middleton Cheney*)

St Agnes of Rome (*c*.291–*c*.304) was a virgin who, according to tradition, was martyred at the age of 12 or 13 during the reign of Diocletian (244–311). Her usual symbol is a lamb (from the Latin for lamb: *agnus*), but here a less frequently used symbol appears – that of a book, suggesting the religious devotion and observance that led to her martyrdom.

Standing to the right and behind St Agnes is another Christian martyr, St Alban. He was said to have been beheaded for sheltering a priest in Verulamium (modern-day St Albans) sometime in the third or fourth century. He is shown carrying the sword with which he was executed, together with a staff.

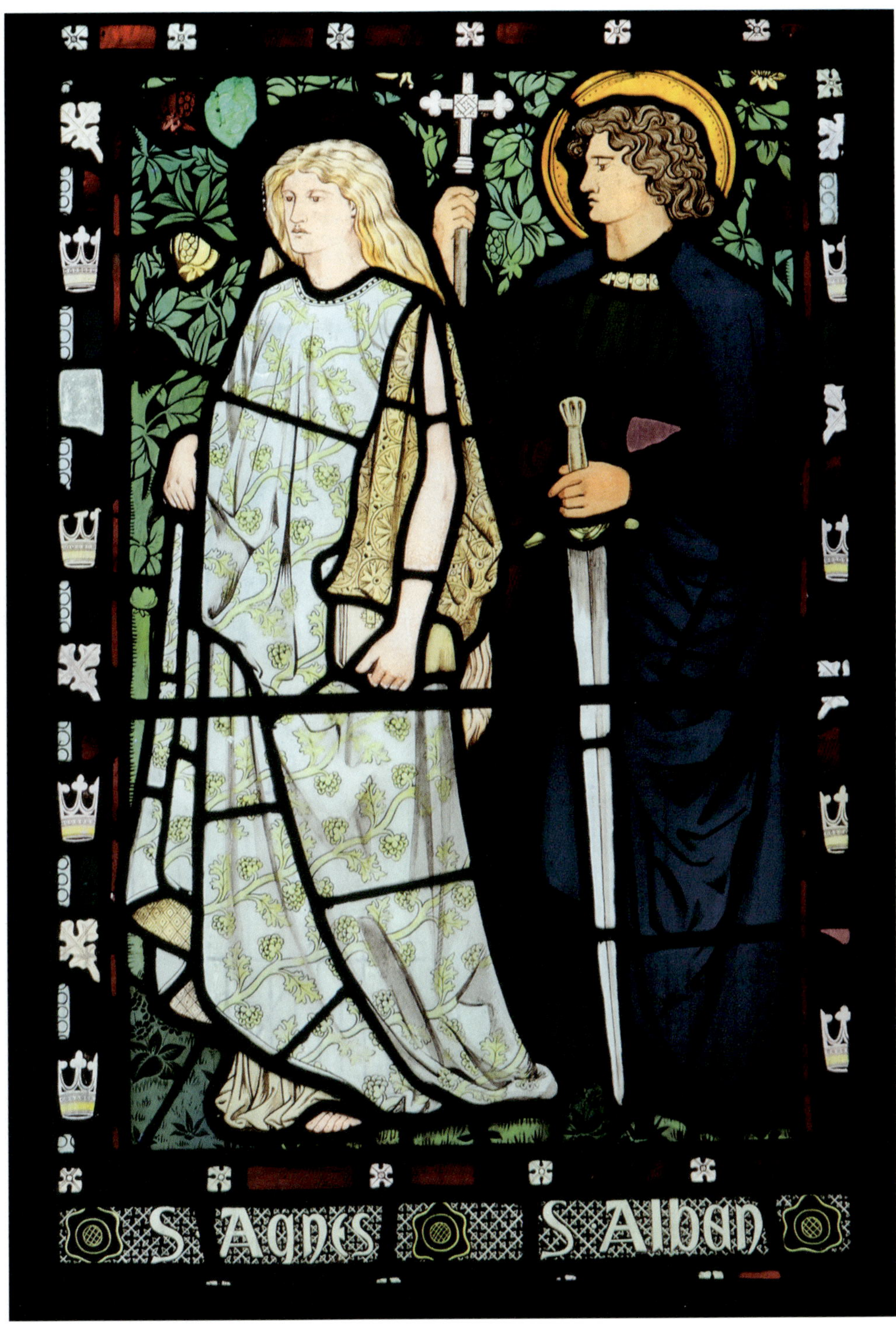

The figures of St Agnes and St Alban from the east window

The beautiful and innovative backgrounds in the figure panels contain foliage (including oak, apple and pomegranate) as well as an array of flowers and plants at the feet of the figures, as the ground they walk upon; stylised versions of recognisable plant-life in a range of greens and blues. The consistent and harmonious use throughout the east window of this stylised flora is a significant factor in the overall unity of the design as a whole. The same is true for Webb's borders of crowns and leaves. The two-dimensional depiction of the backgrounds serves to enhance the three-dimensional quality of the figures.

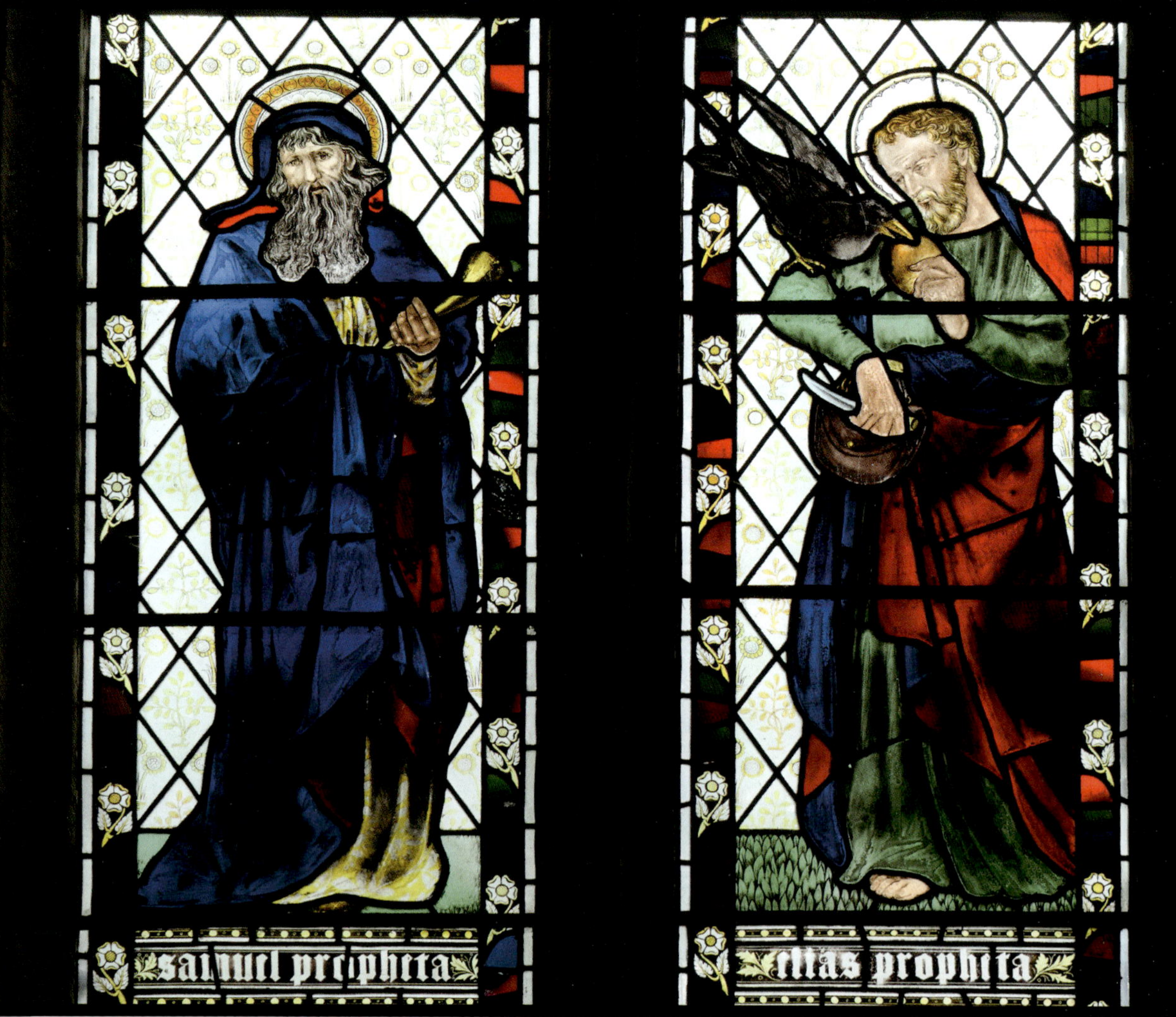

The figures of Samuel (*left*), and Elijah (*right*) from the north aisle north window

2) NORTH AISLE NORTH WINDOW
(designed in c.1866–67, installed soon after)

This two-light Old Testament window has been the subject of some confusion and debate regarding both its date and attribution. In terms of date, the window was probably designed in *c.*1866–67, and installed at All Saints soon after; however, one source gives a much later date of 1880 (*Sewter, 1975*).

The window depicts, on the left, Samuel, the blue-robed prophet. This portrayal is confidently attributed to Edward Burne-Jones who was paid £10 for the work. The design was also used in 1868 at Llandaff Cathedral, Cardiff, and appears in at least 17 other locations.

The window's right-hand panel features Elijah and the Ravens. The story of 'Elias' (as titled here) is told in 1 Kings 17:1–6. Elijah, on predicting a drought, is led to a hide by a spring or brook, where ravens will provide him with bread and flesh in order to survive the severe drought. In this depiction, Elijah appears to be feeding the ravens with bread. This image, with Elijah shown wearing a red cloak lined in blue, has been attributed to William Morris, and appears in a number of other locations, including the Lady Chapel of Bradford Cathedral (1863).

Aside from conflicts over the date, it has been suggested that the figure of Elijah may not be by Morris, but rather by Dante Gabriel Rossetti (*Sewter, 1975*). An insert in the untraced Middleton Cheney Register (post–1877) is said to have recorded Rossetti; however, unlike all the other attributions contained therein, this one was reportedly not later confirmed by a tick. A source of ambiguity is the representation of the figure: the hands and feet are crudely drawn but the rendition of the face is sophisticated, suggesting the possibility that the figure is the work of two artists.

However, while Rossetti had contributed to glass design in the early days of the firm (and produced some 30 designs for the firm in 1861–62), he is recorded as having moved away from the medium by 1864. And as much as we might want the Middleton Cheney Elijah to be by Rossetti, the responsibility would seem to have been that of Morris. Sewter (*1975*) notes of the Bradford Cathedral version that it appears in the firm's Minute Book under Morris's name. The first published attribution to Rossetti may well be in a footnote in *The Buildings of England* volume for the county, published in 1975: 'Mr Glynne Jones suggests Rossetti.' However, the weight of documentary evidence now seems to contradict this attribution.

3) NORTH AISLE EAST WINDOW
(*designed in c.1866–67, installed soon after*)

This three-light window forms part of an arrangement that includes the Horton family pew at this end of the north aisle. A brass plaque under the window in the Horton pew reads:

> In memory of WILLIAM HORTON Esq, late Lord of this Manor and of his wife ELIZABETH; also of three of their sons, JOSEPH, WILLIAM and HENRY GEORGE.

Mary Ann Horton had taken the unusual step of erecting a Gothic tomb in the churchyard, and in November 1865 she arranged for the remains of her father, mother and two of her brothers to be exhumed from the Chapel of Ease at Holloway, Islington in London, and moved to Middleton Cheney where their coffins were placed in the new vault.

The window to their memory was commissioned by Mary Ann Horton, and at least two of the designs appear to have existed in sketch form by *c.*1867. It appears that the windows themselves were probably inserted soon after.

The window depicts, from left to right, St Elizabeth, the Virgin Mary and St Anne. The choice of the figures was deliberate, echoing the names of *Mary Ann* Horton and her mother *Elizabeth*.

The figure of St Elizabeth, mother of John the Baptist, is by Ford Madox Brown, and first appeared in this form at Bradford Cathedral in 1863, with seven further variants, including Middleton Cheney's, appearing thereafter.

The figure of the Virgin Mary, traditionally shown holding a lily for virginity and purity, is by Edward Burne-Jones, and was also initially designed for Bradford Cathedral in 1863, subsequently appearing in a further 12 examples.

The figure of St Anne, the mother of Mary and grandmother of Jesus, is also the work of Ford Madox Brown, and was probably designed in *c.*1868. This is the first appearance of this figure, which was subsequently used in four other locations (including, together with St Elizabeth, at All Saints Church, Coddington, Nottinghamshire). The colour red, symbolic of true love, is traditionally associated with St Anne, and may account for the red rose (also a symbol of true love) that she holds aloft here.

OPPOSITE: The north aisle east window

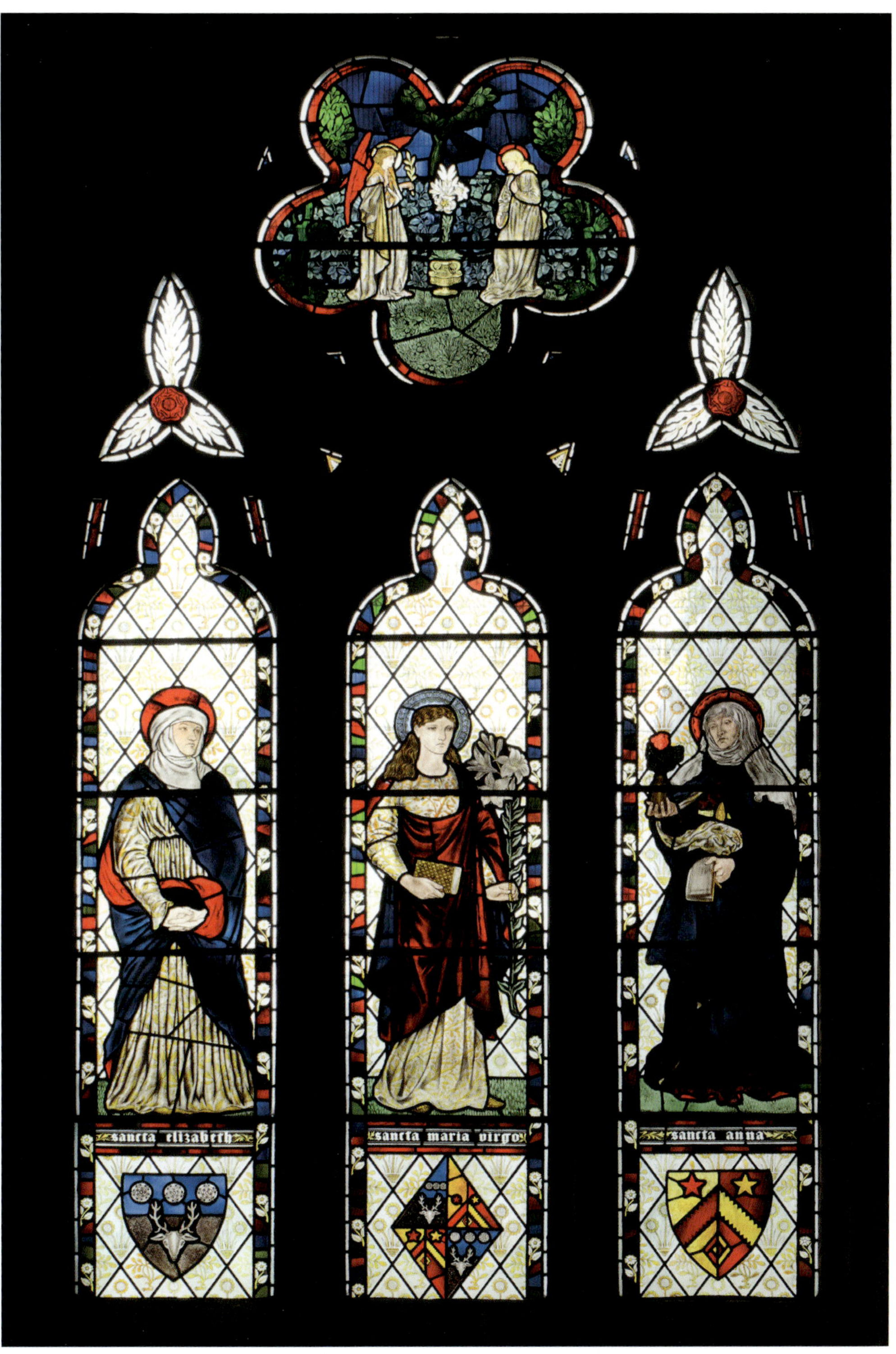
sancta elizabeth
sancta maria virgo
sancta anna

The beautiful cinquefoil (five-lobed) Annunciation light above (*see p. 24*) is by Morris. This design first appeared at the church of St John the Evangelist in Dalton, North Yorkshire in 1868. The Middleton Cheney version dates from 1880 and there are five versions elsewhere. Several versions of this window by the firm are found in their early work for the architect George Bodley who is said to have favoured the subject.

Morris drew the Annunciation for a painted triptych for the church of St Edward the Confessor, Cheddleton, Leek in Staffordshire, and the first design in glass appeared at Lord Leycester Hospital Chapel, Warwick in 1866. Here, in the Middleton Cheney version, a red-winged Angel Gabriel brings the message to a welcoming Mary, standing before an urn of lilies in what could be a nineteenth-century garden setting. The background, rich in stylised plant-life, echoes that found in the panels of the east window – though here takes on a more prominent role, as the figures proportionately fill less of the frame.

The Horton and Sufflee Coats of Arms in the base of the window are by Philip Webb, and the armorials are reflected in the hatchments (painted coats of arms) nearby and above the south aisle, which may have been brought from Islington (or, less likely, created at the time of reburial).

4)   CHANCEL SOUTH WINDOW (*1868–70*)

This window in memory of Ralph Churton, a rector of Middleton Cheney, was installed in the chancel in *c.*1868–70, and is by Philip Webb and Ford Madox Brown. Both Churton and his wife Mary are buried beneath a brass plaque in the chancel floor at Middleton Cheney.

All three upper panels of this window dwell on the theme of 'sacrifice'.

The left-hand panel, by Ford Madox Brown, depicts the sacrifice of a lamb and produce of the field by Cain on the right, and Abel on the left, from Genesis 4. The design first appeared at the church of St Edward the Confessor, Cheddleton in 1866, and was used at a number of other places thereafter.

In the right-hand panel, also by Ford Madox Brown, Melchizedek (King of Salem) offers bread and wine (elements of sacrifice), to Abram (Genesis 14:18). The design, which survives in cartoon form, dates from 1866 and is unique to Middleton Cheney. While studying art in Belgium from 1837–39, Madox Brown may have seen, and been influenced by, an important painting of Melchizedek and Abram by Dieric Bouts the Elder (*c.*1415–75), which

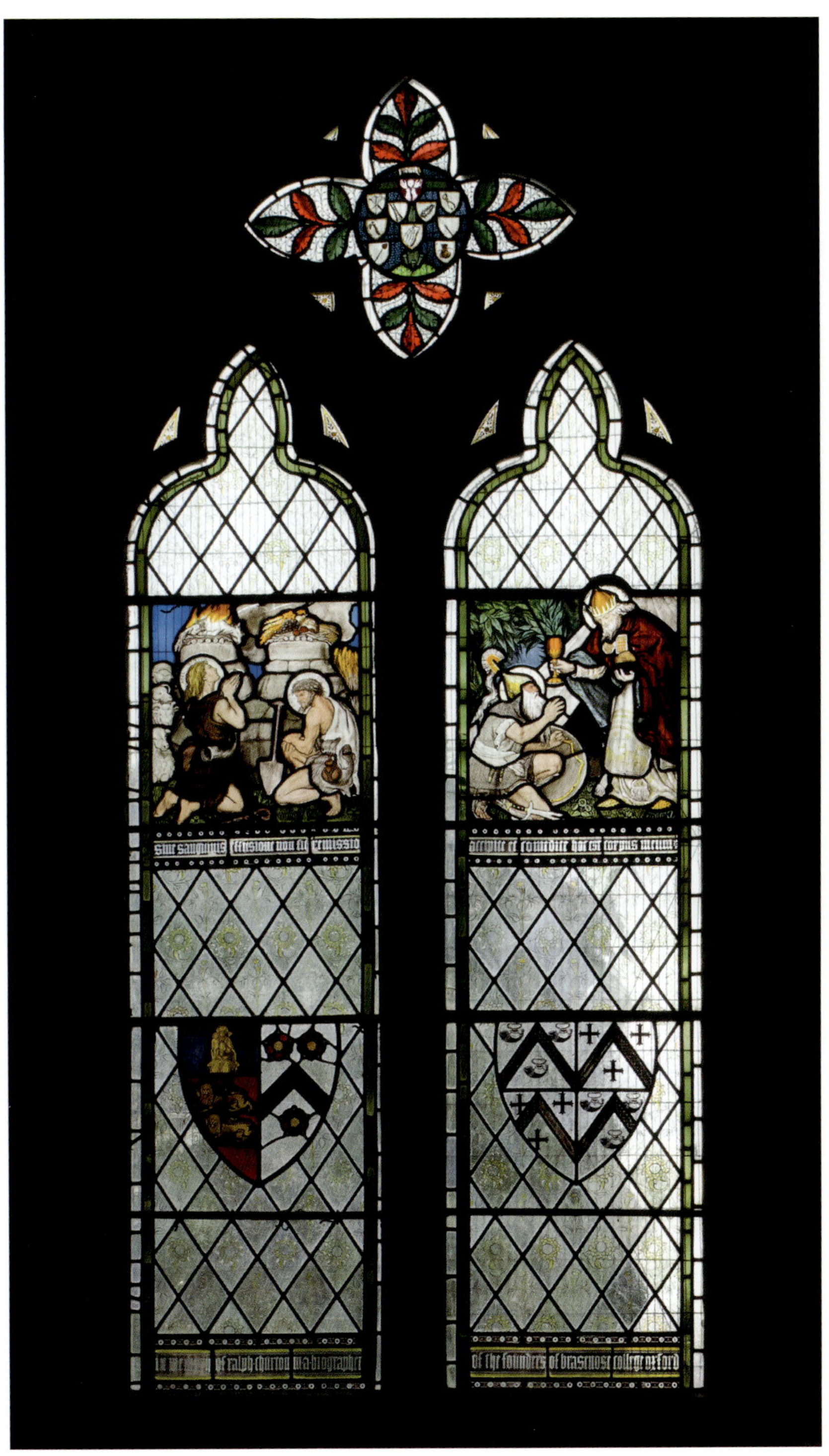

The chancel south window

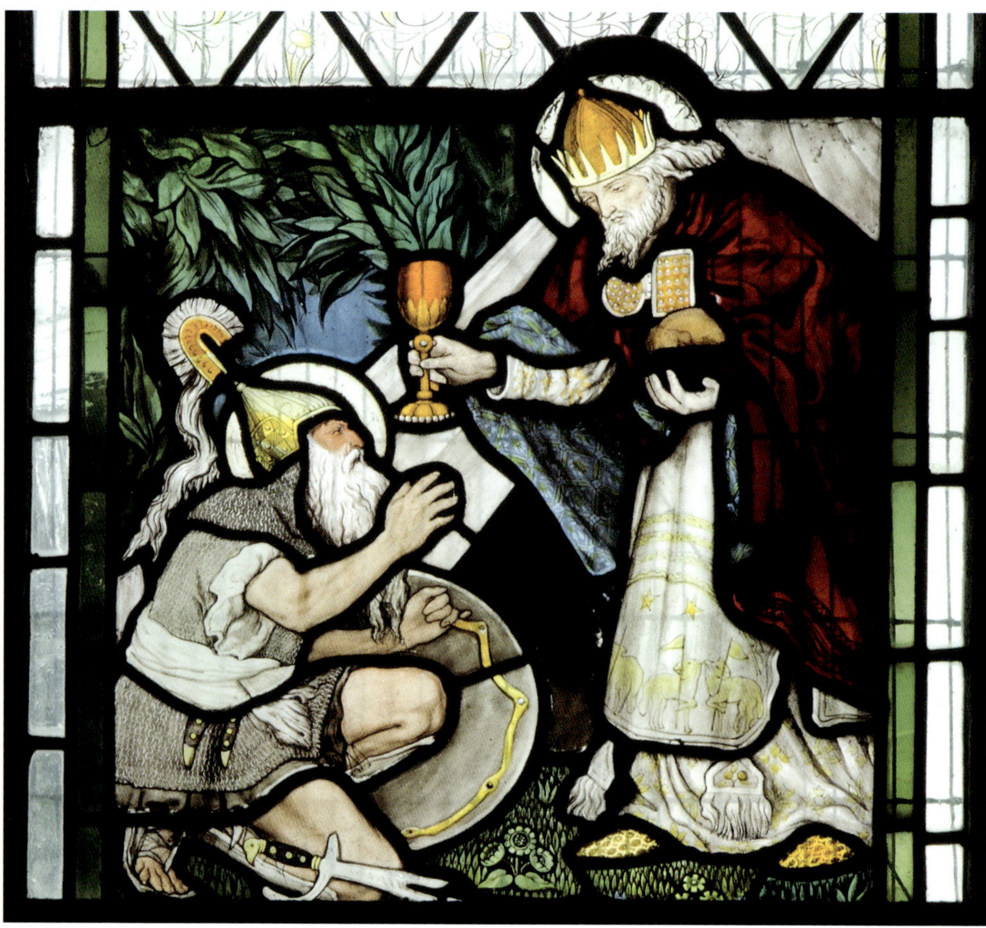

Detail from the chancel south window: Melchizedek and Abram

hangs in Leuven. It has been suggested that the grand priestly garments in this image may reflect the fact that in the late 1860s such traditional Catholic vestments were again finding favour within the Church of England.

The quatrefoil at the top of window is by Philip Webb, and is of 1868–70 (*see p. 74*). It contains nine small shields in clear glass, each containing an Instrument of the Passion. The symbols are: the crossed nails, the hammer, the sponge (with vinegar for Jesus to drink), the ladder (to take down Christ's body), the crown of thorns, the scourge, the pincers, the spear (to pierce Christ's side) and the purse (denoting Judas' betrayal of Jesus for 30 silver coins). This is topped with a tiny medallion in red glass, symbolising the crucified body, containing the symbols of a heart, two spread hands and two feet. Below are shields bearing the arms of the co-founders of Brasenose College, also by Webb.

Born in 1754 at Malpas in Cheshire, Ralph Churton was presented with the living of Middleton Cheney in 1792, and married Mary Calcot of Steane, four miles east of Middleton Cheney. The Churtons had eight children, of whom only four survived Ralph. The theme of this window is sacrifice and forgiveness, and although it was not installed until over 30 years after Churton's death, it seems to be an appropriate choice. His eldest son, wife and two daughters (the youngest being only 14), died within 15 months of each other in 1828–29.

The inscription on the window, from the period 1866–70 reads:

In memory of RALPH CHURTON M.A. biographer of the Founders of
Brasenose College, Oxford.

and

sine sanguinis effusione non fit remissio
accipite et comedite hoc est corpus meum

Churton was a Brasenose graduate and Fellow. Between *c.*1800 and 1810 he had written *The History of the Founders of Brasenose College* (established in 1512), and this window was originally proposed by John A. Ormerod, Brasenose Bursar (1848–64) in 1861.

In a letter, Revd Buckley notes that Ormerod had obtained approval for a contribution of £10 for the window (confirmed in the Vice Principal's Register for 1861), as well as a promise of two guineas from the Senior Fellow, George Hornby. Evidently, there were other promises from the College, all listed in Ormerod's notebook, from which Buckley obtained a copy when he last met Ormerod in Leamington. Ormerod retired in 1864 and died soon after. His executor brother, Arthur, sent Buckley a cheque for all the subscriptions paid to Ormerod and marked off in his book. The College and Hornby subscriptions had not been paid.

Buckley, who wanted the window complete 'by the day of the re-opening, April 19th' (1865) was chasing unpaid promises, an unspecified amount from the Principal, and those of 'a few others'. He was keen to establish cash-in-hand before seeking subscriptions elsewhere. Although it is rumoured that Brasenose College did not ultimately pay for the work, it is likely that misunderstandings surrounding Ormerod's departure may explain much. It would appear, however, that this window was not completed for the reopening.

5) THE WEST WINDOW (*1871*)

The west window was added as a memorial to Mary Ann Horton, and commissioned by her nephew, John Henry Kolle (Horton). Mary Ann Horton (1790–1869) was the daughter of William Horton, a wealthy and successful local landowner and industrialist (noted in particular for his production of elasticated yarn for stockings). Mary Ann endowed the almshouses between Upper and Lower Middleton Cheney on the Main Road, which are still in use, and left money for building the Horton Hospital in Banbury (begun in 1869 and completed in 1872, three years after her death) – with the proviso that there should always be two beds for the people of Middleton Cheney, and that the whole of Middleton Cheney's church spire should be seen from the hospital! She also bequeathed £200 in her will for a memorial window in All Saints Church.

The west window has the following inscription:

> The above window has been erected by the desire and in memory of the late Miss MARY ANN HORTON, Lady of this Manor and last surviving child of the late WILLIAM HORTON Esq of Highbury, Middlesex who departed this life on the 19th July 1869 aged 79 and is interred in the burial ground of this church.

The west window was designed by Edward Burne-Jones alone in 1870 (as noted in his account book of July that year), and was installed in 1871. It is generally known as 'The Fiery Furnace', though it has also been referred to as 'The Three Holy Children' (*Sewter, 1974*), and this was its first installation. It is widely regarded as one of the most effective windows in Burne-Jones' mature style, and illustrations for this window further helped to establish Burne-Jones' national and international reputation. The window is now much-lauded by art historians, not least because the swirling flames anticipate the next major art movement to take hold in Britain – Art Nouveau in the 1890s.

In terms of its overall structure and subject-matter, the west window comprises three related elements: the Fall of Adam and Eve (Genesis 3), the Six Days of Creation (Genesis 1:1–2:3) and the story of the Fiery Furnace from which three Jews from the court of Nebuchadnezzar were saved by God. The three elements are linked by the themes of creation and redemption.

OPPOSITE: The west window

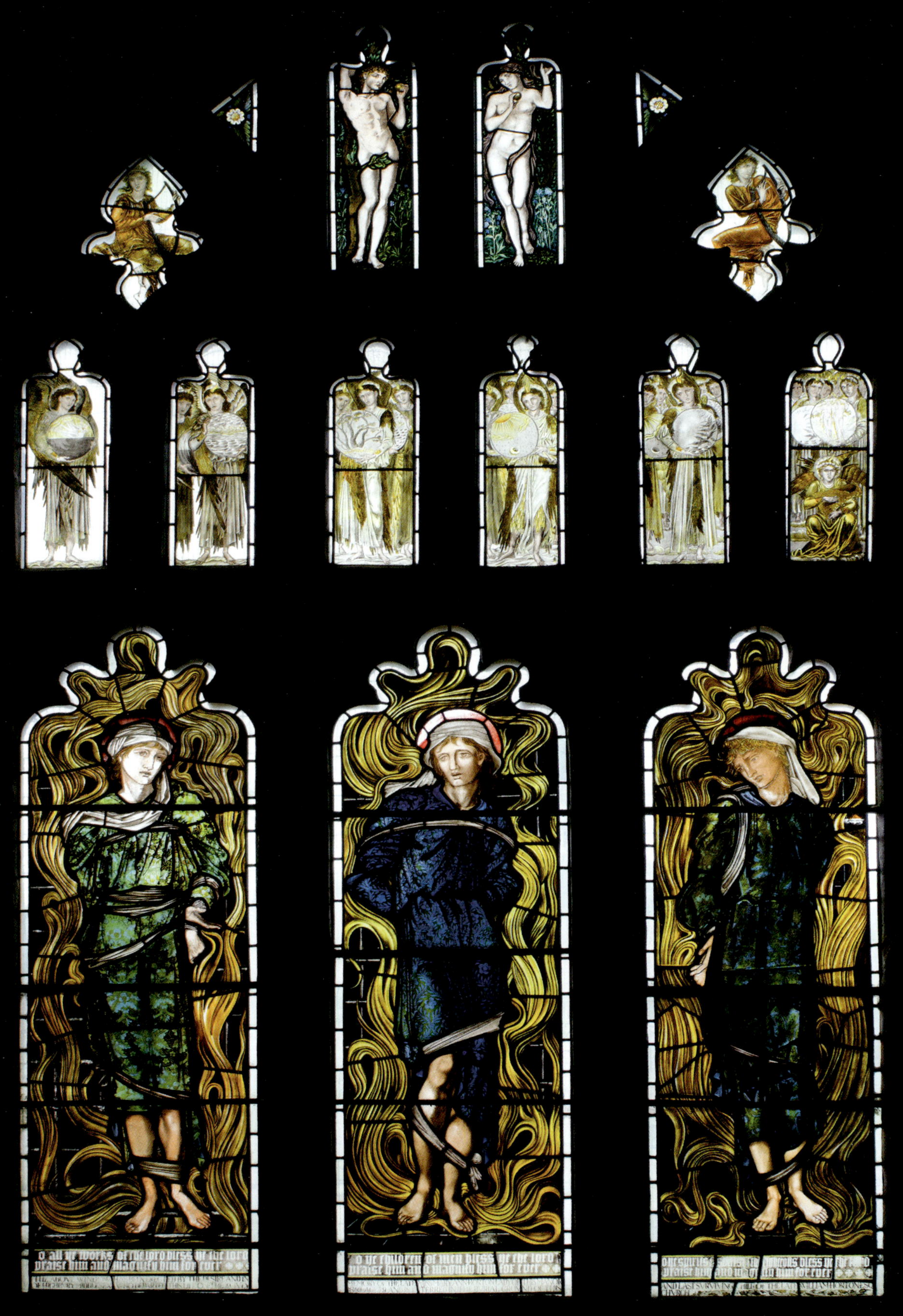
O ALL YE WORKS OF THE LORD BLESS YE THE LORD
PRAISE HIM AND MAGNIFY HIM FOR EVER
O YE CHILDREN OF MEN BLESS YE THE LORD
PRAISE HIM AND MAGNIFY HIM FOR EVER

ADAM AND EVE

The sinuous *contrapposto* figures of Adam and Eve are both depicted holding golden apples, against a richly decorated background of flowering plants. The figures were designed in 1870, with related drawings for Adam and Eve now in the Victoria & Albert Museum. Burne-Jones' notes adjacent to the figures' legs went as follows: '… put millions of flowers here as in the foregrounds of good women … Gerard's herbal all over here …' – clearly indicating his aspirations for the decorative surround.

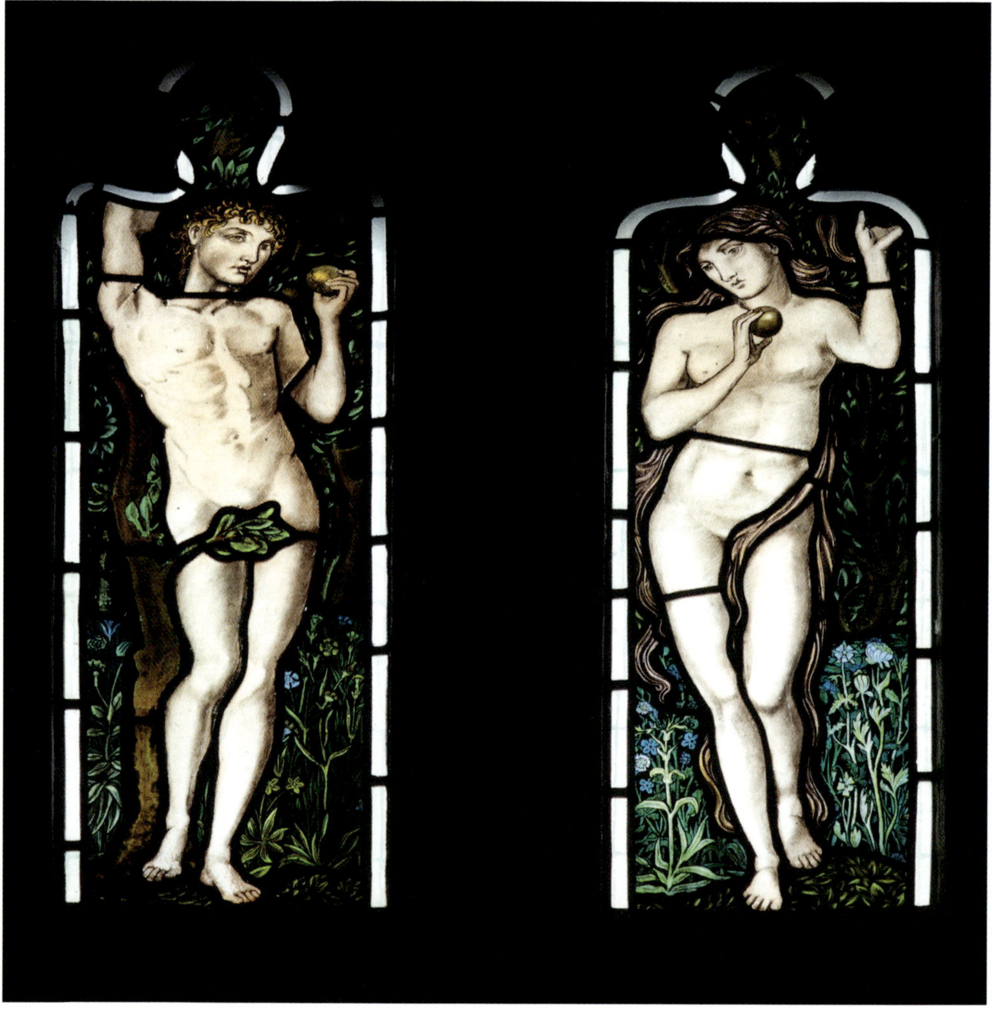

The figures of Adam and Eve, from the top of the west window

The two angels clad in golden-brown garments, playing harps, are shown as if seated or floating in mid-air. The figures were designed by Burne-Jones in 1870 (the cartoons are now lost).

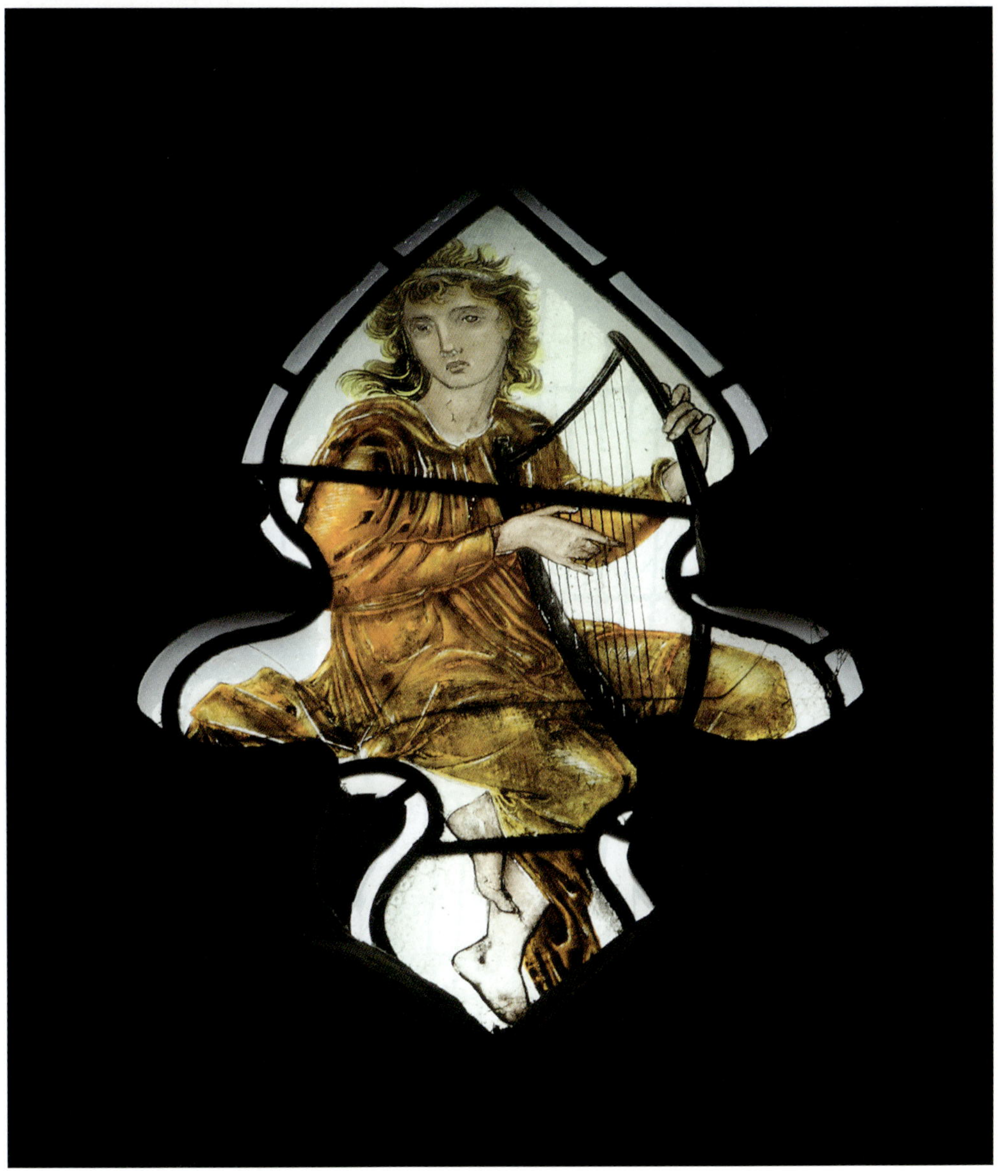

One of the two angelic musicians from an upper light of the west window (*see also p. 65*)

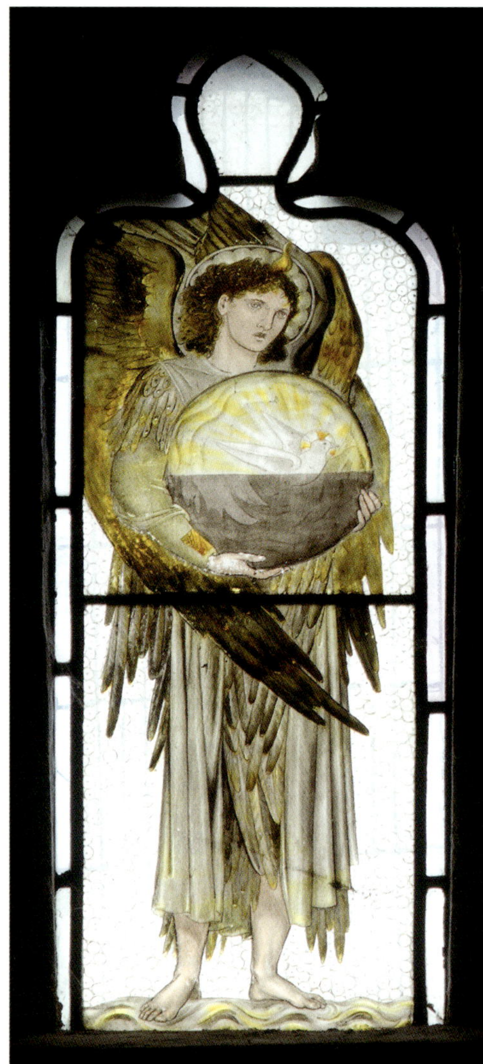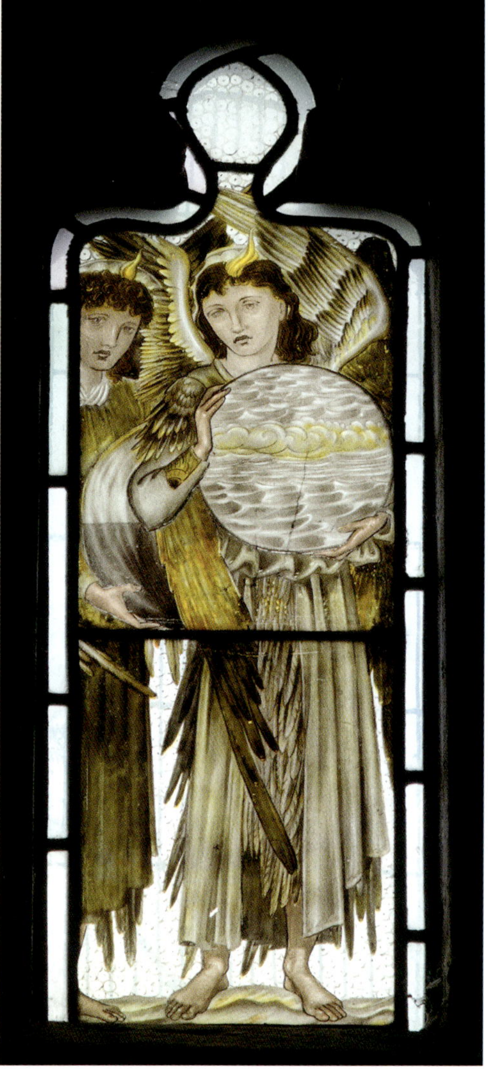

The Six Days of Creation/ The Angels of Creation, from the west window (*panels 1 and 2*)

THE SIX DAYS OF CREATION/ THE ANGELS OF CREATION

Designed by Burne-Jones in July 1870. The design concept, of a series of panels each depicting an angel holding a disc-like globe, and with the number of angels increasing from one to six from left to right, has no historical precedent, and is regarded as marking a major change in Burne-Jones' style as it evolved during the 1870s.

The globes depict, from left to right, the Creation story taken from the book of Genesis: 1) the creation of the light; 2) the creation of the firmament; 3) the

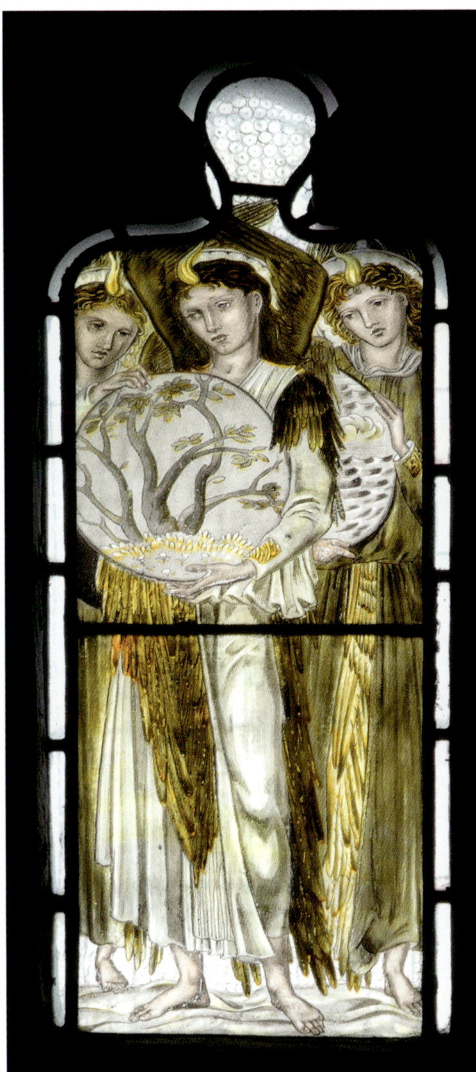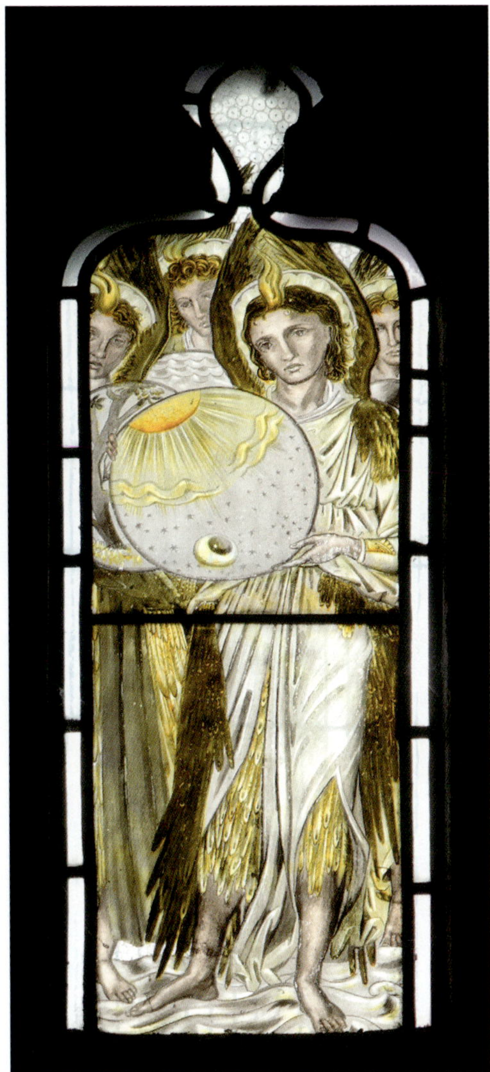

The Six Days of Creation/ The Angels of Creation, from the west window (*panels 3 and 4*)

creation of the dry land; 4) the creation of the lights in the firmament (including the sun and moon); 5) the creation of living creatures; 6) the creation of man. With each successive panel, a new creation event is brought forward by an angel who stands in front of those that have gone before. In the last frame, on the right, is a seated angel holding a psaltery or zither, indicating that on the seventh day God rested.

Burne-Jones later pursued the theme of the Six Days of Creation, first with a more detailed set of pencil drawings begun in 1871, then with a larger set of

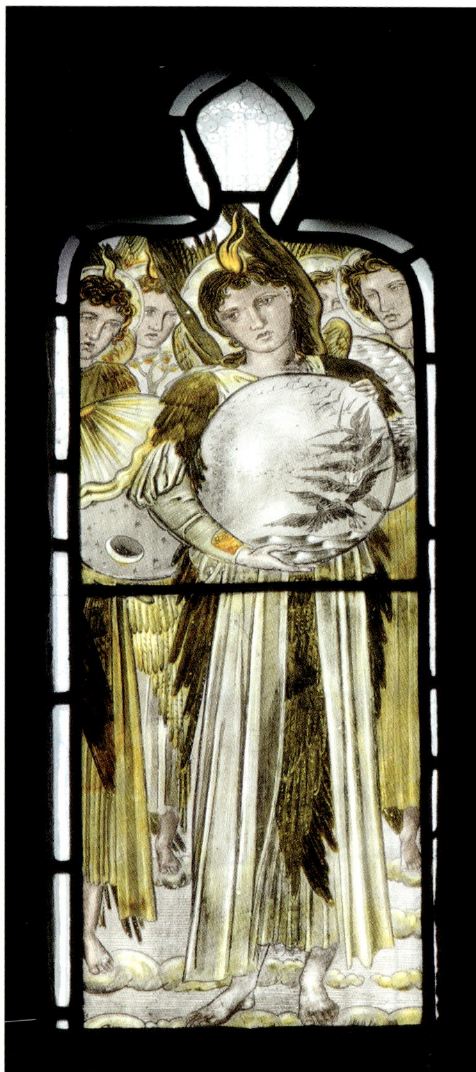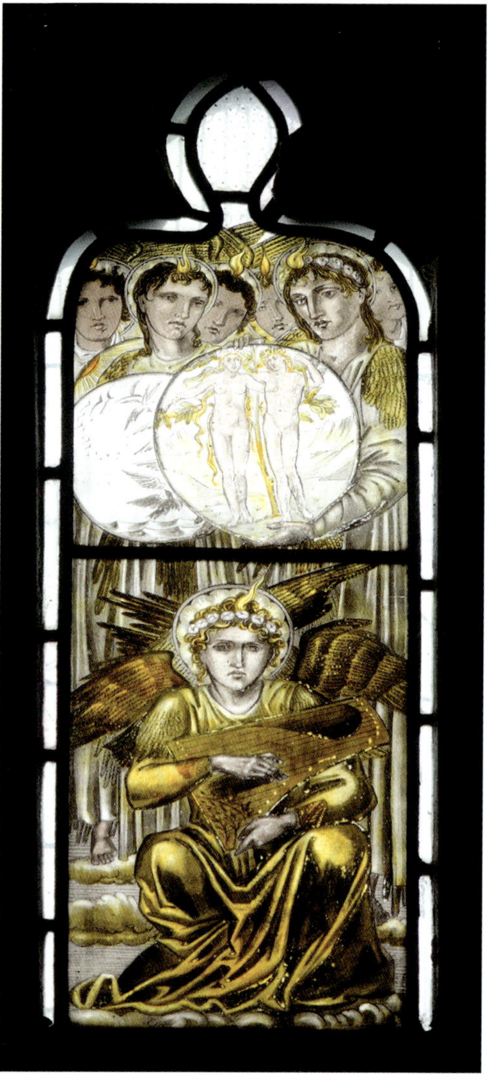

bold gouache watercolour images embellished with gold and platinum paint, and mounted in a Renaissance-style frame designed by the artist. This group of paintings was prominently exhibited at the Grosvenor Gallery in New Bond Street, London in 1877, triggering much critical discussion – including by John Ruskin, who was complimentary of the series; and in an article by Oscar Wilde, subsequently included in that author's *Miscellanies*.

This exhibition, in the year of the Gallery's opening, inspired Gilbert and Sullivan's reference to 'Greenery-Yallery' in their light opera, *Patience*: a reference to Burne-Jones' affluent Aesthetic supporters – 'the Souls'. The comment was an allusion to the deathly pallor possessed by many of the figures in the paintings, with the relevant verse running:

> *A pallid and thin young man,*
> *A haggard and lank young man,*
> *A greenery-yallery, Grosvenor Gallery,*
> *Foot-in-the-grave young man!*

The author Henry James was fascinated by the faces of the Angels of Creation, and by what he termed, 'that pathos, that appealing desire for an indefinite object, which seems among these artists an essential part of the conception of human loveliness'.

Despite (or perhaps because of) the satirical and critical debate that took place, the Grosvenor exhibition established Burne-Jones as a major artist of the avant-garde, with one writer noting that, 'the reclusive artist had been transformed, uneasily, into a cult figure of his period' (*McCarthy, 2012*).

The Six Days of Creation designs appear elsewhere, having been translated by William Morris from cartoon to stained glass – including in the Church of St Editha, Tamworth in 1874, and much later in the Chapel of Harris Manchester College, Oxford in 1896. This latter (and much larger) series is more highly coloured, with red-winged angels holding glass marble-like globes; the line-work and colouring characteristic of later work produced by the firm. A striking later version – this one conceived as a series of highly-glazed ceramic panels – was created in 1893–1906 for the Dyfrig Chapel at Llandaff Cathedral.

The pencil cartoons were given by Burne-Jones to his friend and muse Aglaia Carnonio. They have remained in private ownership ever since, though came up for auction in 1974 and again in 2013 (with a sale estimate of $40,000). Burne-Jones also turned the drawings into a set of larger, more elaborate paintings. These have hung in the Harvard Fogg Museum collection since 1943 – less the fourth panel (the emergence of the sun, moon and celestial bodies) which was stolen and has not been recovered. Burne-Jones had wanted the paintings to stay together as a coherent narrative in one frame, but this huge frame was regarded as unwieldy when it arrived in America so it was broken up, regrettably making the work vulnerable to theft.

The major element of the west window in terms of the size and prominence of the imagery is the Fiery Furnace depicted in the three main lights. The subject-matter is taken from the book of Daniel (1–3), and continued in part of the Apocrypha, book of the Three Holy Children. In the story, Shadrach, Meshach, and Abednego refused to worship a golden statue, so were thrown into the fiery furnace by King Nebuchadnezzar. They went into the furnace singing and praising God. The singing continued, and on looking into the furnace, the king saw four figures, as an angel had been sent to protect the men.

The 'Furnace' element of the west window has generally received less critical attention than the 'Creation' panels above – despite the innovative treatment of the subject-matter, and their marking of an early stage in the creative journey that would culminate in the four massive pictorial panels produced by Morris and Burne-Jones for St Philip's Cathedral, Birmingham between 1884 and 1897.

Taken in isolation, the three beautifully-rendered figures might not stand out from other similar figures in glass by the firm at this period. However, the extraordinary treatment of the flames – here envisaged in swirling, almost hair-like or ribbon-like golden tendrils – arguably does more than any other single element in the west window to compel the attention of the onlooker.

Burne-Jones' decision to depict the flames in this way has enabled the artist to make the best possible use of the available glazed space, and to respond most effectively to its constraints, with the tendrils, for example, looping around the lobes at the top of each light. Here, with the graphic and stylised treatment of the flames, Burne-Jones seems to have been particularly attuned to how the window might have visual impact when seen from distance – for example when looking west from the entrance to the chancel (in contrast to the smaller and more intimate panels of the Creation series above, which invite closer scrutiny). Additionally, Burne-Jones has cleverly exploited the west-facing aspect, the golden rays of evening setting suns making the flames vividly alight.

This window design was installed in only one other place: St Luke's (formerly St Wilfrid's) Church in Farnworth, now part of Widnes in Lancashire, in 1875/6. In this later version, the figures are paler and appear in a different order. Studies for two of the furnace figures, entitled 'Azarias' and 'Ananias', survive in the Lady Lever Gallery on the Wirral. Although the 1870 cartoons of the Furnace are untraced, they are recorded in Burne-Jones' Account Books.

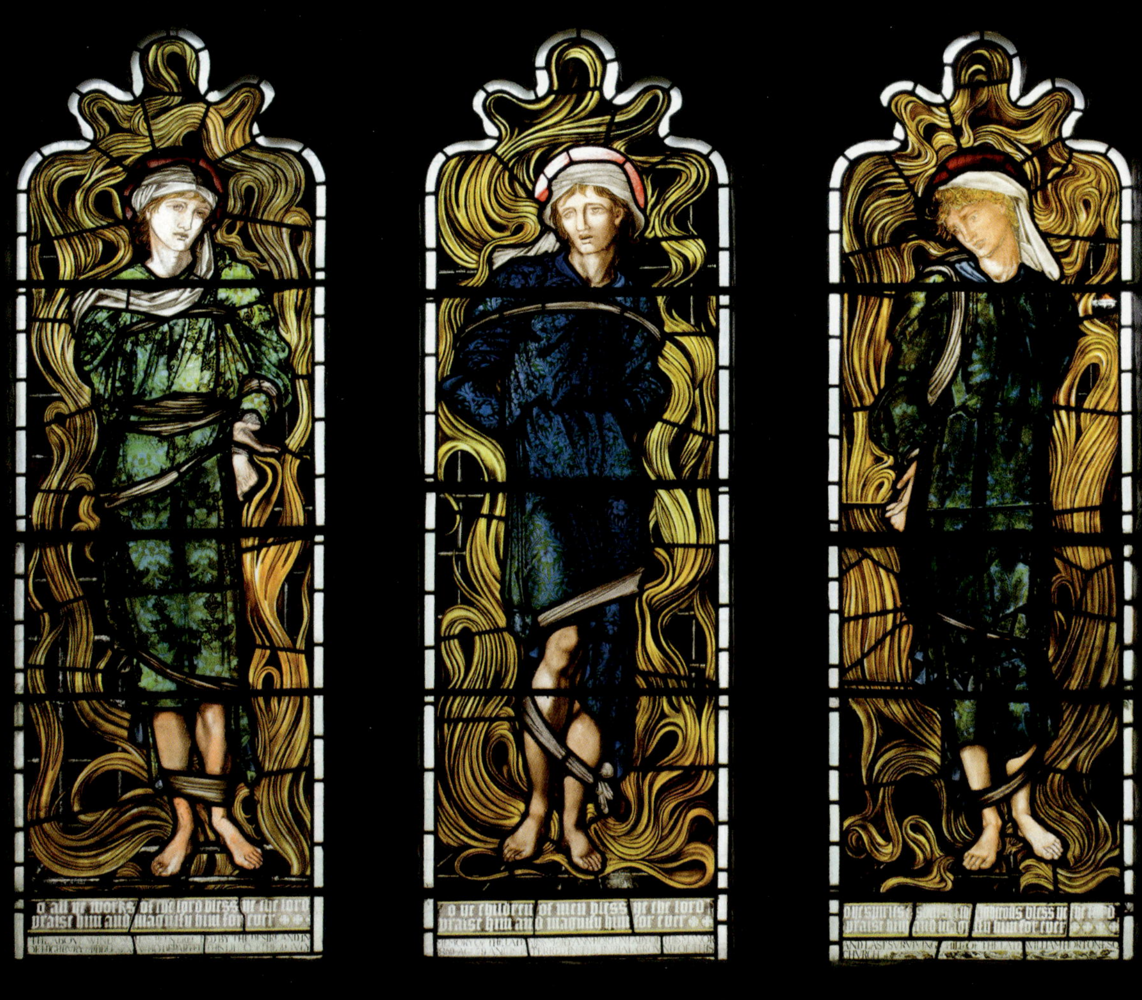

The three principal lights in the west window, depicting the Fiery Furnace

The Fiery Furnace was an enduring artistic theme in the nineteenth and twentieth centuries, including for J.M.W. Turner whose picture of the subject was exhibited at the Royal Academy in 1832, and is now in Tate Britain. 'The Burning Fiery Furnace' (Op 77) of 1966 was also one of *Three Parables for Church Performance* by Benjamin Britten, and is one of the three themes used by twentieth-century stained glass artist John Piper (1979) in his north aisle memorial window to Britten in the Church of St Peter and St Paul at Aldeburgh, Suffolk.

With the exception of the Buckley memorial, this was the last of the Morris & Co. windows to be installed at Middleton Cheney, and remains not only one of the most striking windows created by Edward Burne-Jones, but one of the finest stained glass windows of the nineteenth century to survive anywhere. It is generally acknowledged that from the middle-1870s onwards there was a decline in the quality of Morris & Co. glass, with more design and manufacturing delegation as Morris's interests moved elsewhere. The Morris style was taken up by other manufacturers and designers, as the next two windows illustrate.

6)   THE GABLE WINDOW (c.*1871*)

The gable window, high above the chancel arch, was inserted in 1871 (*see p. 63*). Philip Webb's account book for September 1870 records, 'arranging dove for Middleton Cheney … 5s'. In a dynamic arrangement that cleverly exploits the encircled trefoil of the tracery frame, the Dove is depicted in an earthward dive (John 1:32: 'I saw the spirit descending from heaven like a dove').

Webb had included a more complex image of a similar subject at the head of the Rose Window at All Saints Church, Selsley, Gloucestershire in 1861, and the various components were also 'arranged' for the head of the window featuring St Elizabeth and St Anne at Coddington, Nottinghamshire.

7)   SOUTH AISLE EAST WINDOW (*1885*)

This is another memorial window, with a brass inscription recording the names of six members of the Croome family: 'MARTHA, JOHN, SARAH, ROBERT, JAMES and ANNE'.

The windows portray St Luke (with a book) and St James (with a locked book and substantial wooden club, a traditional symbol of martyrdom). Robert Croome was listed as a Member of the Royal College of Surgeons, and qualified in 1815, becoming a pioneer in the use of the smallpox vaccination, so it can surely be no coincidence that the Croome family chose St Luke, the Patron Saint of Physicians and Surgeons for one of their windows. Luke is portrayed as 'the beloved physician' (Colossians 4:14). He carries a large volume of his works, and the tiles have inkhorns and quills. The border surrounding St Luke includes his associated symbol of an ox or bull.

The windows are by John William Brown (1842–1928) and Murray Bernhard Bladon (1864–1939). They were manufactured by the firm of Powell and Sons (Whitefriars Glass). Brown may have worked with Morris & Co. before working as an 'outside artist' with Powells, for whom his major work was the *Te Deum* window at Liverpool Anglican Cathedral. Bladon, meanwhile, became better known as a painter.

8) SOUTH AISLE WEST WINDOW (*1891*)

This too is a memorial window, this one to one of Middleton Cheney's former churchwardens, Charles Brickwell (baptised 1811; died 1889). Along with Revd Buckley, Brickwell applied to Peterborough Diocese for the faculty to restore the church in the 1860s. The inscription for the window records the names: CHARLES JOHN BRICKWELL, ELIZA his wife and ELIZA FRANCES, their daughter.

The window, dated 1891 in Powells' books, depicts St Andrew (with a saltire cross) and St John the Baptist (making a blessing and holding a cross-topped staff). It was designed by George Woolliscroft-Rhead (1855–1920), who was trained in painting by Ford Madox Brown, and was described in 1890 as a Pre-Raphaelite. A painter, etcher and designer of stained glass and ceramics, Woolliscroft-Rhead belonged to the mainstream of the Arts and Crafts movement and was an apprentice at Minton and Co., a member of the Art Workers Guild and an 'outside artist' for Powells.

9–10) CHANCEL NORTH WINDOWS (*1893*)

These two windows were inserted in memory of Revd William Buckley, the rector of Middleton Cheney, who oversaw the church's restoration in the 1860s. The associated wall plaque is inscribed:

> To the Glory of God and in memory of the Revd W E BUCKLEY MA,
> formerly Fellow of Brasenose College Oxford and for 38 years Rector of
> this parish. These windows the gift of the parishioners and numerous other
> friends were dedicated on St Philips and St James's Day 1893. 'Whosoever
> liveth and believeth in me shall never die'.

The window designs were said to be chosen by Buckley from the catalogue of Edward Burne-Jones, and were possibly designed in consultation with Buckley.

The rector left instructions in his Will that the parishioners were to raise the money to pay for the windows! The archives show that over £140 was collected by a committee led by T.W. Eydon who had latterly moved away to Eydon Hall. The windows were dedicated on May Day 1893, with Revd C. Hebberden, Principal of Brasenose College, amongst those attending.

An account of the dedication service notes that,

> There was a very large number of children present, each little one carrying a bouquet of flowers, and it is worthy of remark that the whole of the Nonconformist denominations in the village united in the service and in doing honour to the memory of one who was beloved by all.

The windows were produced in 1893, and show events from the life of Jesus (*see pp. 16–17 and p. 71*). *The four panels of the western window depict*:

1. THE NATIVITY, with the baby Jesus asleep, an exhausted Mary and, seated to the right of the child with a doting expression, Joseph; the family group screened and overseen by a protective angel. This panel was originally designed in 1873 for Jesus College, Cambridge (a cartoon for the design survives in a private collection).

2. ADORATION OF THE MAGI, with the three wise men or kings (traditionally Melchior, Caspar and Balthazar) kneeling in prayer before the infant Christ (*see p. 84*). The panel was also designed in 1873 for Jesus College, Cambridge, and was used in ten other locations (a cartoon for this design also survives in a private collection).

3. CHRIST IN THE CARPENTER'S WORKSHOP, with the young Christ clad in red, dutifully planing (note the curled shavings on the floor), while Joseph works a chisel. The activities are overseen by an angel playing a psaltery (*see p. 72*). The scene was designed in 1874 for the church of St Mary the Virgin, Speldhurst, Kent, and appears in 13 other places.

4. CHRIST AMONG THE DOCTORS, with the young Christ identified here, as in the other three panels of this window, by his halo with a red cross. As with the above panel, this too was designed in 1874 for the church of St Mary the Virgin, Speldhurst in Kent. This image is known from nine further examples.

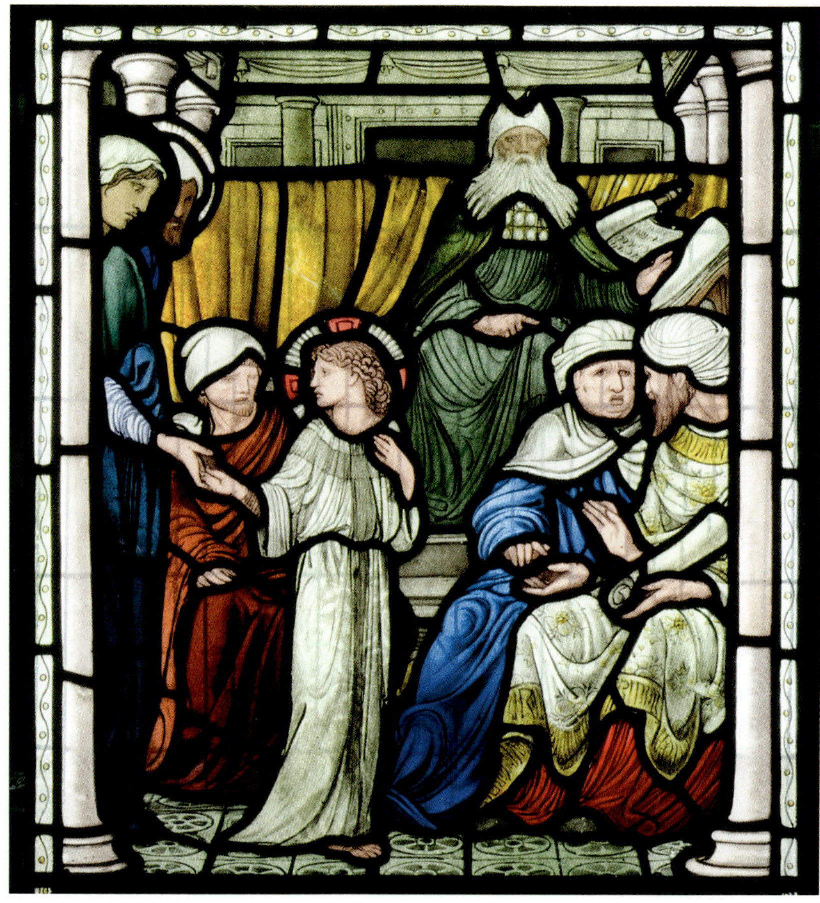

Christ among the Doctors, from the chancel north window (west)

The four panels of the eastern window depict:

I. **BAPTISM OF CHRIST**, with Christ in the rippling waters of the Jordan, head bowed before John the Baptist, and surrounded by angels. This is another design of 1874, originally for St Mary the Virgin, Speldhurst in Kent, and appears at a further 14 locations.

2. **THE RAISING OF LAZARUS**, with the striking figure of Lazarus beginning to undo the strips of linen that make up his grave clothes – as witnessed by, among others, Lazarus' sister, Martha. This was designed by Burne-Jones in late 1877, originally in different colours, for St John of Beverley, Whatton. It appears in only one other location (Forfar, 1881) and is known from a cartoon now in the National Gallery of Canada.

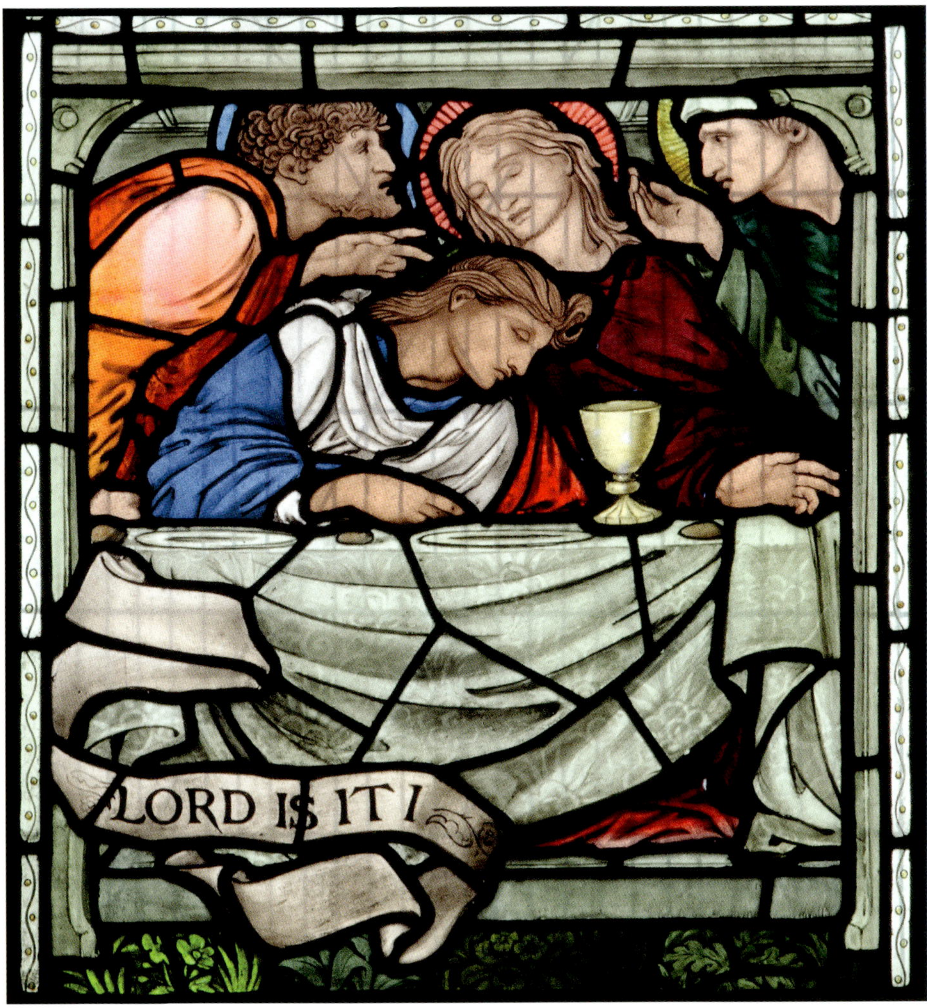

The Last Supper, from the chancel north window (east)

3. THE LAST SUPPER, dealing specifically with the betrayal of Judas, and the Disciples crowding in to ask, 'Lord, is it I?' This was designed in 1872 for the Lady Chapel of Christ Church, Oxford, appearing in six other locations. The foliage strip at the base of this panel is of the same type as that found through-out the east window, and may have been an addition, or filler, by Morris.

4. ENTOMBMENT OF CHRIST, with the naked and lifeless figure of Christ being carried by Joseph of Arimathea to the rock-cut tomb, prior to being wrapped in linen for His burial (*see p. 73*). This was designed in 1876 for the Church of St Martins in the Bull Ring, Birmingham, and no other example is known. A cartoon for the design survives in Bristol City Art Gallery.

4

Fruit of the Earth and Work of Human Hands

A spiritual, theological commentary on the glass in All Saints, Middleton Cheney

FRUIT OF THE EARTH AND WORK OF HUMAN HANDS

THESE words are often used at the preparing of the altar in the Eucharist, where they refer to the bread and wine, but they might also be used of any work of art. For works of art use natural materials which are then made into something else, just as grain which has grown from the earth is milled and the flour made into bread. The coloured glass windows in churches are themselves made of material stuff: glass, lead and paint. These things have to be made from raw materials. Glass, for example, is made from melting sand, and the use of various minerals gives the colour. So, iron oxide gives a blueish green, calcium a deep yellow, cadmium and selenium give reds and oranges. The techniques for doing this were being rediscovered in the early to mid nineteenth century. Eighteenth-century glass was, by and large, made by painting on glass, but William Morris (who made most of the windows in this church) and others decided to go back to recreate the techniques and style of medieval glass. Light itself, although it seems the least material of things, is in fact a physical thing, and it is the combination of light and glass that gives these windows their most attractive qualities.

The window maker, then, has the raw materials from which the window is to be made. A design is created, and a full-size cartoon made. Then the pieces of glass are carefully cut to fit with the lead to make the mosaic of the window. The lead is shaped so that the glass fits into it. What may surprise people is that in this church several artists were responsible for each window: the background panels, the borders, and the figures are often by three different people. And rarely are the designs unique. Glass studios created catalogues of windows, just as other firms made catalogues of pulpits,

61

pews, vestments and so on. The designs of some of the Middleton Cheney windows were chosen from a catalogue, and others were used in varied forms elsewhere. This is partly because there was a huge increase in commissions for new windows in the nineteenth century. It was a boom industry.

These windows are, therefore, fruit of the earth, in that they use natural materials, all part of the created order, and thus a gift from God. They are also the work of human hands, not only in the manufacture of glass, lead and so on, but also in the design and making of the final product.

There is an image of the Church here too. St Paul wrote of the Church as the Body of Christ, how it is made up of many members, and how each member is essential for the whole. In 1 Corinthians 12:27 he writes, 'Now you are the Body of Christ and individually members of it.' It is an organic image, the working together collaboratively of each to make the whole. And this we see in the many hands involved in the creation of the windows: commission, design, production, and lots of people involved at every stage. So then, it is a reminder of how the Church works as a body of people, each with their own vocation, but all together being the Church. This might seem self-evident, but as we look at these windows we are invited to reflect on their corporate qualities.

In the Eucharist, the bread and wine are to become the Body and Blood of Christ, in which we receive the divine life. This is what the Prayer Book calls a 'means of grace' in the General Thanksgiving. The windows can also be a means of grace, and it is to that end that this commentary is written.

THE HOLY SPIRIT

High up on the east wall of the nave, above the chancel arch, is a small window with glass by Philip Webb (1870). It is the Dove Descending. It is where we begin our tour of the windows because the Dove represents the Holy Spirit. The dove has a long history as a religious symbol. In ancient near-eastern religions the dove represented the goddesses of fertility and procreation, among them Astarte and Venus. In the Bible, in the story of Noah (Genesis 8), as the waters begin to recede, Noah sends out a dove. The first time it simply returns; the second time it returns with an olive leaf in its beak, and the third time it does not return. So the dove became a symbol of peace and God's goodwill. Doves were also offered in sacrifice, so that when Jesus is taken on his 40th day by Mary and Joseph for his presentation in the Temple, they take a pair of turtle-doves (Luke 2:24). But the most important use of this image is at the Baptism of Jesus, where the Holy Spirit descends on him in bodily form like a dove.

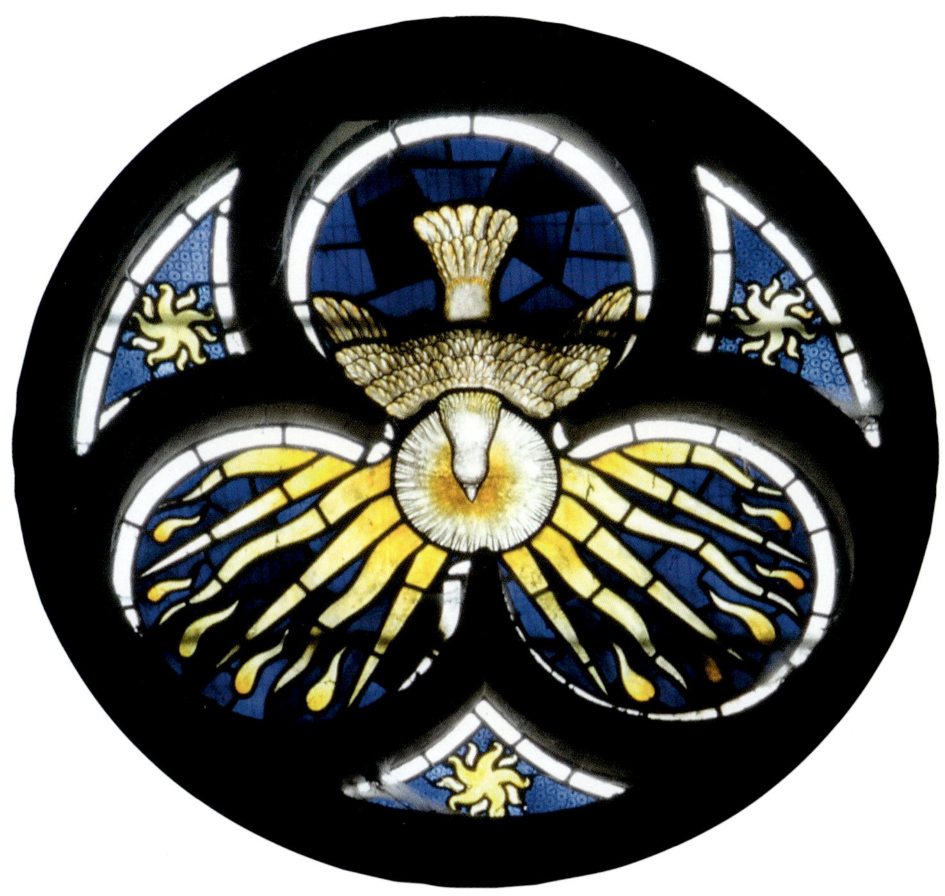

The Dove Descending, in the gable window above the chancel arch

The dove was widely used in art as a symbol of the Holy Spirit. We see it in Annunciations, in images of the Trinity, and in the coming of the Spirit at Pentecost. In the first few Christian centuries the dove was a potent but hidden symbol for Christians generally. The Cross only came into prominence in the fourth century when Christianity was no longer proscribed.

The Church is formed by the Holy Spirit. He is sent by the Father at the intercession of Christ at Pentecost. He is the Lord, the giver of life, as the Nicene Creed puts it, the one who energises and vivifies the Church. He is the one through whom Christ becomes present among us. He is the advocate (*see John 14*).

I think the fact that this window is not one we immediately see is significant. We have to look up; we have to search for it. But more often than not we probably come upon it when we don't expect it, and that speaks strongly to us of the Spirit's activity among us. Perhaps, as we are invited to 'Lift up our hearts', we might look to this image, mindful that we are asking the Spirit to be with us.

The dove, then, is a symbol of peace, of the creative and life-giving qualities of God, the one who dwells in our hearts, the source of our whole being.

THE BENEDICITE WINDOW (EDWARD BURNE-JONES 1870)

At first sight this window in the west wall of the tower seems to tell three stories: the Six Days of Creation (Genesis 1:1–2:3), the Fall of Adam and Eve (Genesis 3) and the story of the three Jews at the court of Nebuchadnezzar being saved by God in the burning fiery furnace (Daniel 3 and The Song of the Three Holy Children in the *Apocrypha*). But theologically they tell one story: creation, redemption and the praise of God. The elements all hold together in God's redeeming love.

In this west window the images of the creation, with angels holding discs with the activity of each day on them, are said to be unique to Burne-Jones, although much copied since. The number of angels increases day by day, showing the cumulative work of creation. The Genesis story uses the cosmology of its day, and we should not read this as science. The important points are that God creates; He is the source of all that is. The creation is ordered and purposive. The ancient Antiphon for the Magnificat on 16 December speaks of the divine Wisdom – 'sweetly ordering all things'. It is the work of the Trinity: the Father – Creator of heaven and earth, of all that is, seen and unseen; the eternal Word – through whom all things were made; and the Holy Spirit – the Lord, the giver of life. We see the unseen in the angels, who are not mentioned in Genesis. Our time patterns are a result of the creation

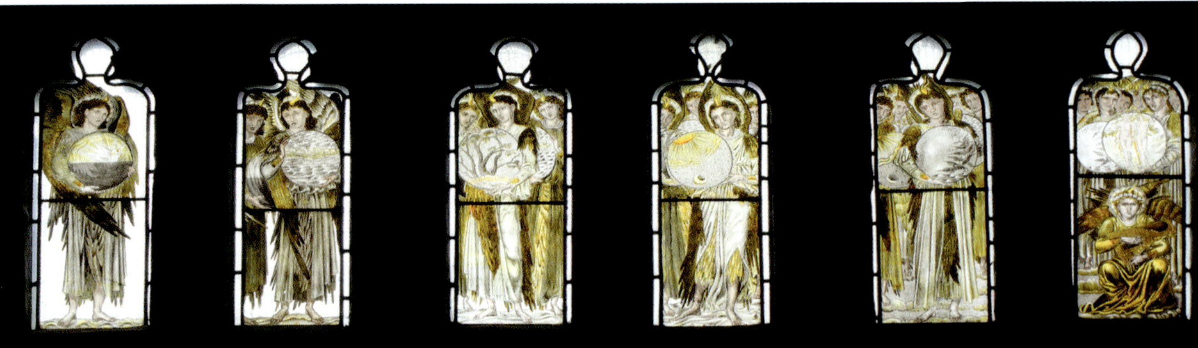

The Six Days of Creation lights in the west window (*see also pp. 50–52*)

story: seasons, day and night within the overall design of the universe, but also the week, Sunday to Saturday. Six days for work and the 'Sabbath' for worship and rest. For Christians, the day of Resurrection is the first day of the week. In the figure of Day Six there is also a seated seraph playing a psaltery, and above are two angelic harpists. So here we have music, which for many centuries was a symbol and reality of design and a source of delight and joy; and, therefore, perhaps an image here of the seventh day.

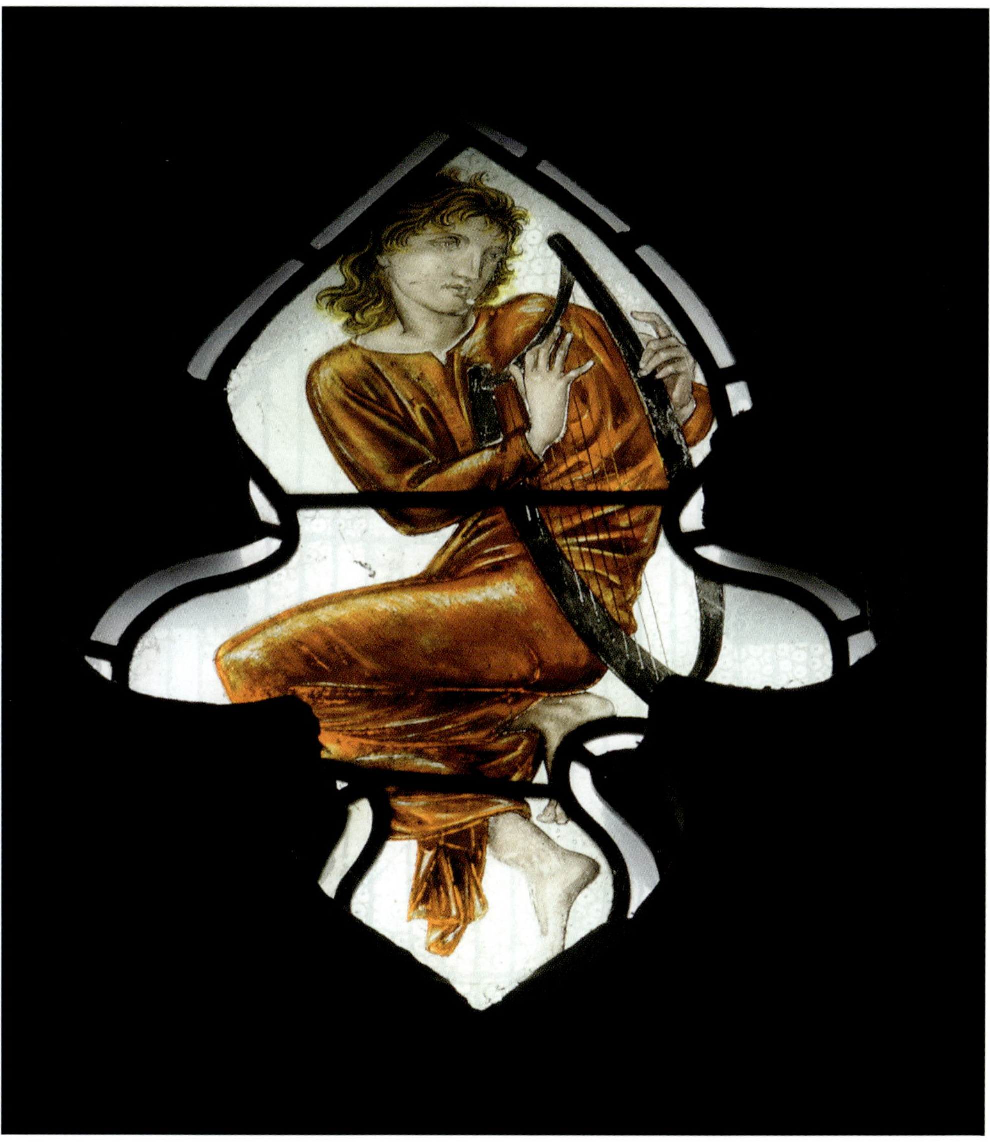

Harp-playing angel in one of the upper lights in the west window (*see also p. 49*)

The phrase that reverberates in the Genesis story is that God saw what he had made and it was good. And on the sixth day 'indeed it was very good' (Genesis 1:31). We need to hang on to that when we are looking at our world. God's creation is very good; but then we look up and we see Adam and Eve in the garden from which they are about to be expelled. This shows us humanity with its God-given freedom but with its waywardness, its disobedience, its self-centredness and its tendency to cause pain and sorrow. That reality is imaged by the story in Genesis 3, which seeks to explain how a very good creation becomes the world as we know it, with its strata of goodness, beauty, truth, joy and love, but interleaved with strata of sin and death.

That truth is also imaged in the burning fiery furnace. This is the story of the Jews in exile in Babylon under King Nebuchadnezzar, in the sixth century BC. The Exile itself was seen as a punishment for sin, for a turning away from God to the false gods, and of not living the ethical way which the Torah invited them to live; living instead with injustice, idolatry, and empty worship. So now they find themselves a subject people in a very alien culture. However, Daniel himself and these three young men, Hananiah, Mishael and Azariah, come to prominence in the Babylonian society. They are given new names – a not uncommon practice of tyrants to distance people from their own identity, culture and religion. So as Shadrach, Meshach and Abednego, they flourish until the great image of Merodak is created, and they are required to fall down and worship the image. When they refuse, Nebuchadnezzar, in his anger, has them thrown into the furnace. You notice here the contrast with Adam and Eve, who are disobedient, with the three men who are faithful to God. The bound men are then seen by the king to be unbound, walking around in the fire and unscathed by the flames, and there is among them a fourth man who 'has the appearance of a god' (Daniel 3:25). But before this, there is an insertion into the original Hebrew text. The insertion is in Greek and thought to have been written in the second century BC by an Alexandrian Jew. It begins with a long prayer of penitence, and then the three sing with one voice a hymn of praise. We know this as the Benedicite. It has long been used in the daily prayers on Sundays, and remains there in the *Roman Office Book*. When Cranmer was compiling the *Book of Common Prayer* in 1549 he made it an alternative to the *Te Deum* in Lent. It is now in Common Worship as a canticle for Morning Prayer. It is this prayer that we see in the principal light of this window. Below is part of the text: *O all ye works of the Lord praise ye the Lord. O ye children of men, praise ye the Lord* and *O ye spirits and souls of the righteous, praise ye the Lord.*

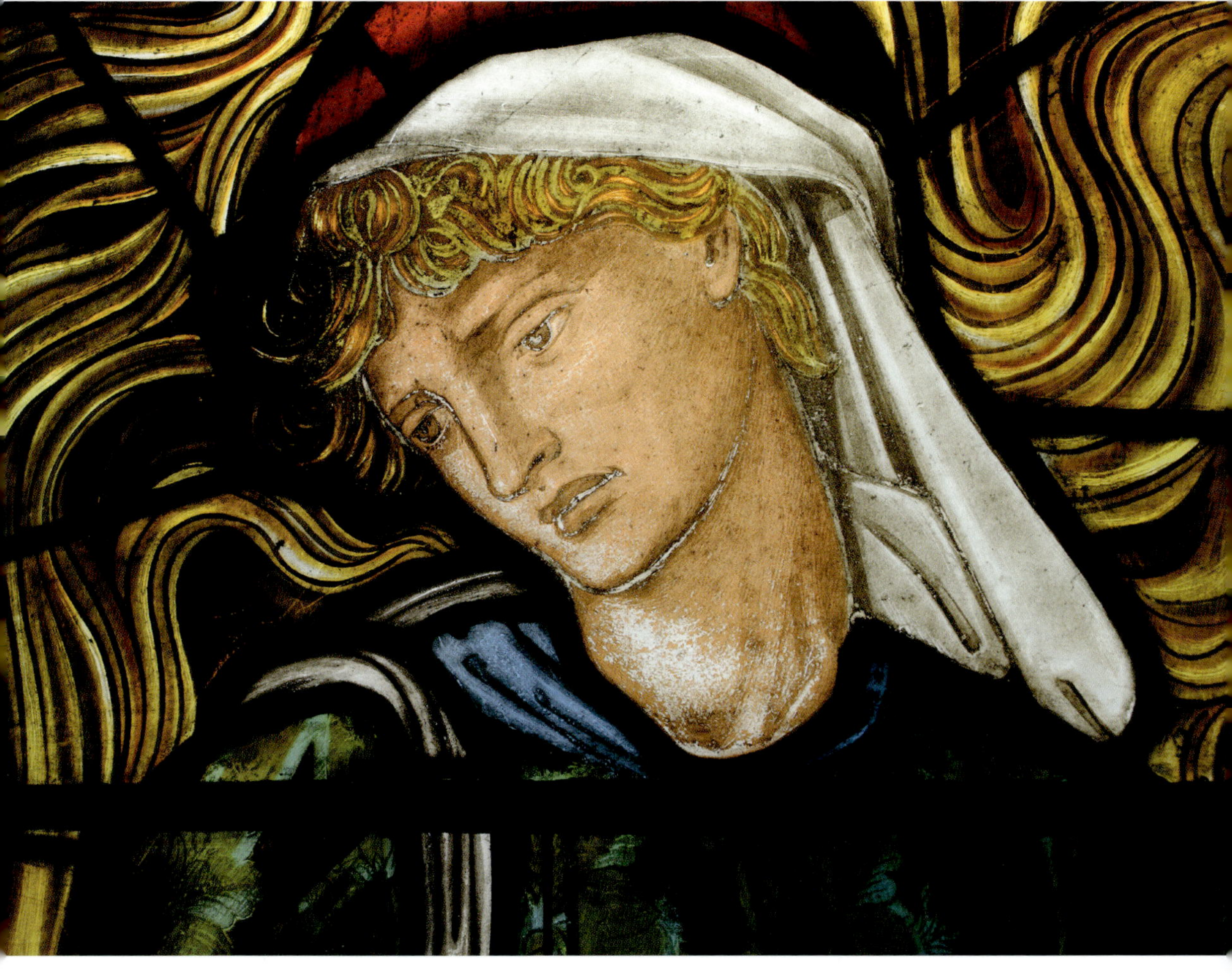

The figure of Abednego in the west window (detail)

If you examine the whole text you will see that the first part is about the heavenly creation, the second about the earthly creation and the third part is about humanity. Only humanity can articulate the praise of the creation, but everything else praises God by its very being.

The figures of the men in their green-blue robes with touches of gold, make a strong contrast with the flames moving, curling and rising around them. The fire is, to me, the hard circumstances, the pains and hurts and confusions of life. But humanity in its right relationship to God, in penitence and praise, comes through unscathed because of the presence of Christ among us. This window gives us hope that 'all manner of thing shall be well', as St Julian of Norwich wrote.

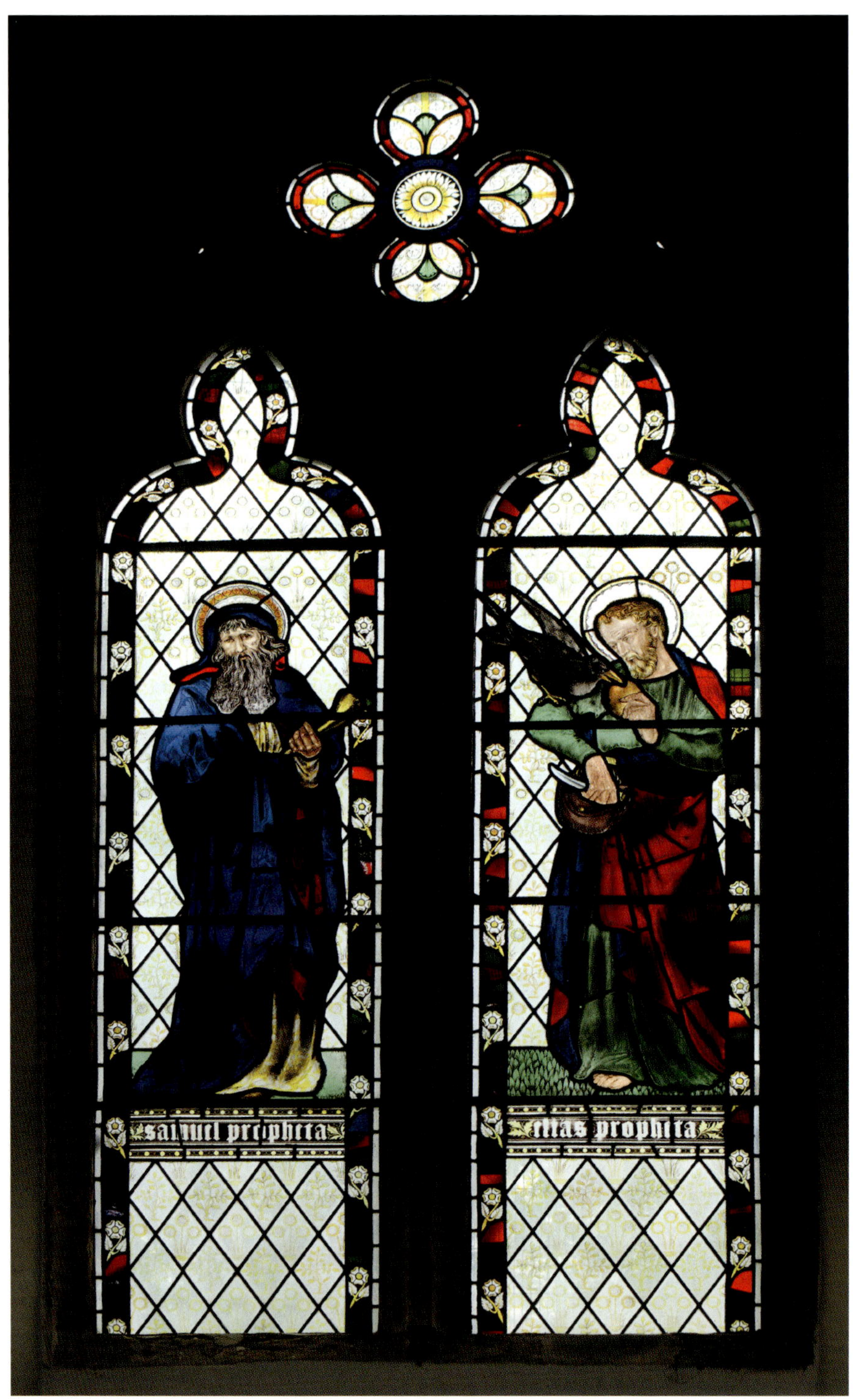

The figures of Samuel and Elijah in the north aisle north window

The belief that the Word of God became a man, which we call Incarnation (the 'enfleshment'), is at the heart of Christian theology, and in the north aisle of the nave we find images that are leading towards it. There are images here of Samuel and Elijah, both of whom are described as *propheta*. We find their stories in 1 Samuel and in the books of Kings (1 Kings 17ff). The figures are set above quarries with plants, and there are borders of roses. You will see a lot of plants in these windows; however, they are rarely identifiable as specific species. They have that Arts-and-Crafts expressionism, but of course they speak to us of the natural world. Elijah has a pouch and a knife and he seems to be feeding the raven with a circle of bread. You will remember the story of how, during a time of famine, Elijah was fed by ravens (1 Kings 17:1–7). This circle of bread in the window reminds us of the bread of the Eucharist.

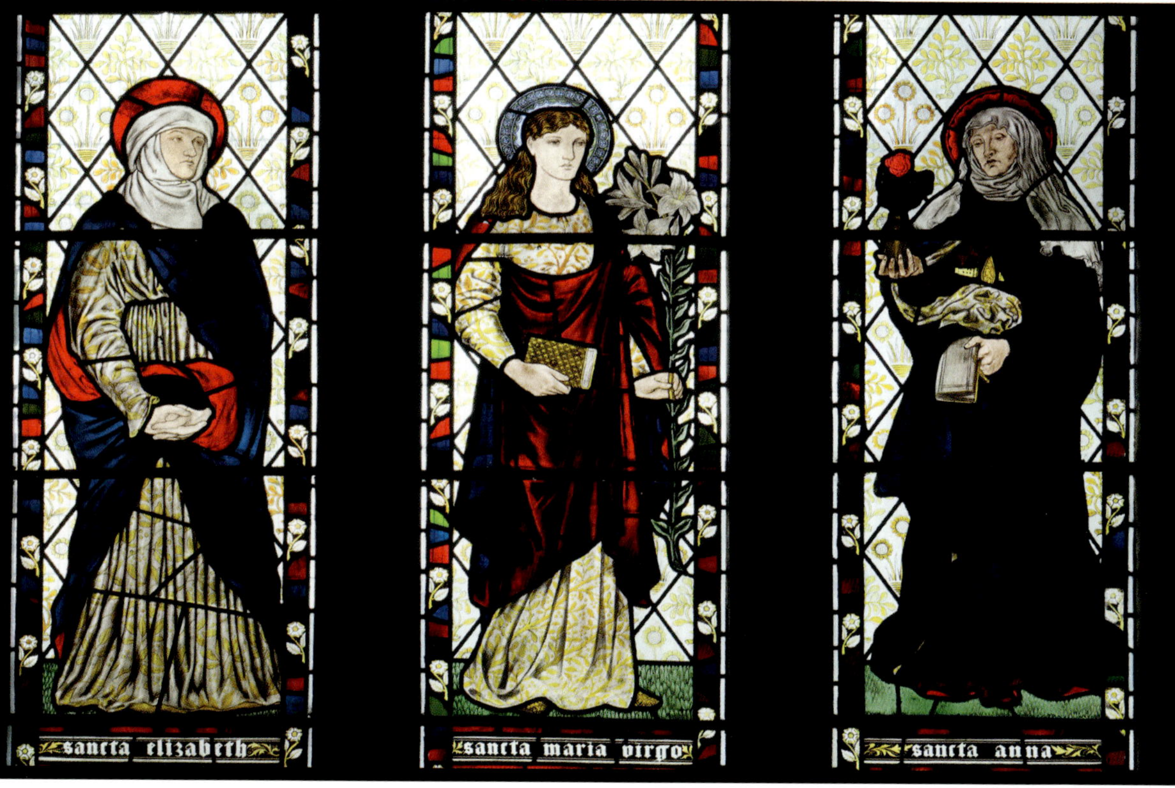

The figures of Saints Elizabeth, Mary and Anna in the north aisle east window

In the east wall of the north aisle is a further composite design: St Anna and St Elizabeth are by Madox Brown; St Mary was designed by Burne-Jones; the Annunciation is by William Morris and the shields by Philip Webb. The lower part of the window sets the scene for the encounter of Mary with Gabriel in the window above. Mary stands in the centre: she has a blue halo, long hair and holds both a book and a lily. These images speak of her purity, youth and devotion. The book in these images is always a prayer book. To either side are the Saints Elizabeth and Anna. Anna is Mary's mother, according to the apocryphal Gospel, Proto-James. Luke's Gospel tells of Mary's cousin Elizabeth who becomes the mother of John the Baptist. The language of flowers is important here: myrtle and rose. The myrtle represents love and marriage, and the rose is also about love. The lily denotes humility, devotion and chastity.

The Annunciation is set in a garden: a flowery mead, trees and the pot of lilies. This image has been a constant in paintings and glass since early medieval times. Here, Morris contrasts the garden of obedience with the garden of disobedience of Adam and Eve. Mary's inclined head speaks of her 'Yes' as she responds willingly and lovingly to God's desire that she be the mother of the eternal Word. Gabriel has wonderful red wings and the figures stand out by the intensity of the glass.

In Elizabeth, Anna and Mary we see three women looking forward to hope for the redemption of God's people. They are like Simeon and another Anna in Luke's Gospel: this small group of faithful Jews through whom God acts. They are devout, attentive and willing to respond positively and joyfully to God's activity among them. We don't see the Visitation here, but we can recall the visit of the newly pregnant Mary to her cousin Elizabeth, also pregnant, who declares: 'Blessed is she who believed', and Mary sings her Magnificat.

In the north wall of the chancel are windows designed by Burne-Jones. These were from his catalogue; in other words these were not designed for this church, and the designs are repeated in other places.

They take forward the imagery of Jesus' life: the Holy Family, the adoration of the Magi, the Carpenter's workshop and Jesus as a boy in the temple. In the second window we see the Baptism of Jesus, the raising of Lazarus, the Last Supper and the Burial of Jesus. These windows were chosen by William Buckley, and we can see that his choice falls into two groups: the childhood of Jesus and his Ministry. The Holy Family reminds us of the key role

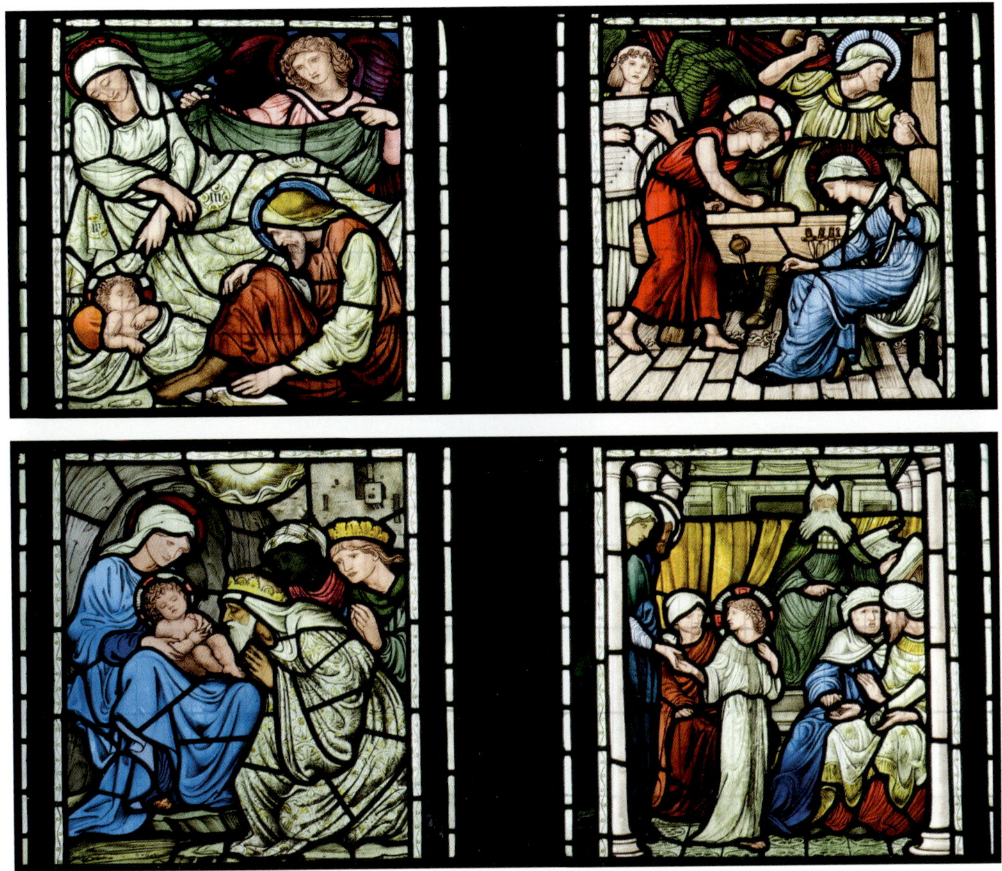

Chancel north window (east) showing scenes from the life of the infant Christ

both Joseph and Mary had in those first years: Joseph the one who guards mother and child and takes them to Egypt. This is underlined by the choice of the Magi rather than the shepherds. It was the Magi's visit to Herod which brought about Herod's fury and the massacre of the young boys of Bethlehem. The tradition of showing the three Magi with the Child and Mary reflects the words of St Matthew, and the three men are shown as coming from different generations and races: one is young, another old and the third is black.

The Gospels tell us that Joseph was a carpenter. The nineteenth-century artists, and especially the movement we know as Arts and Crafts, and of which Morris was the instigator, loved the simple craft in wood – this was the natural, non-industrial craft that this movement encouraged. So, in the windows there are shavings on the floor, the tools are evident. Mary sits on a stool watching. Jesus is learning to plane, and Joseph is about to bring down his mallet. It is a domestic scene and its perfection, as Morris and his colleagues saw it, is emphasised by the music: an angel is playing a psaltery. So, it is not only divine music but ecclesiastical: psaltery clearly having some etymological connection with psalm. They are both derived from the Greek word for 'to pluck' – psalms being texts sung to a plucked accompaniment.

There is no biblical story of Jesus the carpenter, but one story of his childhood is told by St Luke in which, after a visit to Jerusalem, Jesus is eventually found with the teachers in the Temple. For this, Burne-Jones shows a classical, columned building. We see the high priest with a scroll and two figures on the right arguing a point, again over a scroll. The scrolls are, of course, the Jewish scriptures and the 'arguments', the questions and answers, are about the interpretation of these texts. We see the moment when Jesus is acknowledging the authority of his parents, as he puts his hand out to Mary's hand. But the Lukan text reminds us of his growth in wisdom and stature, and Mary's pondering on these things. We too are invited to ponder on the Incarnation.

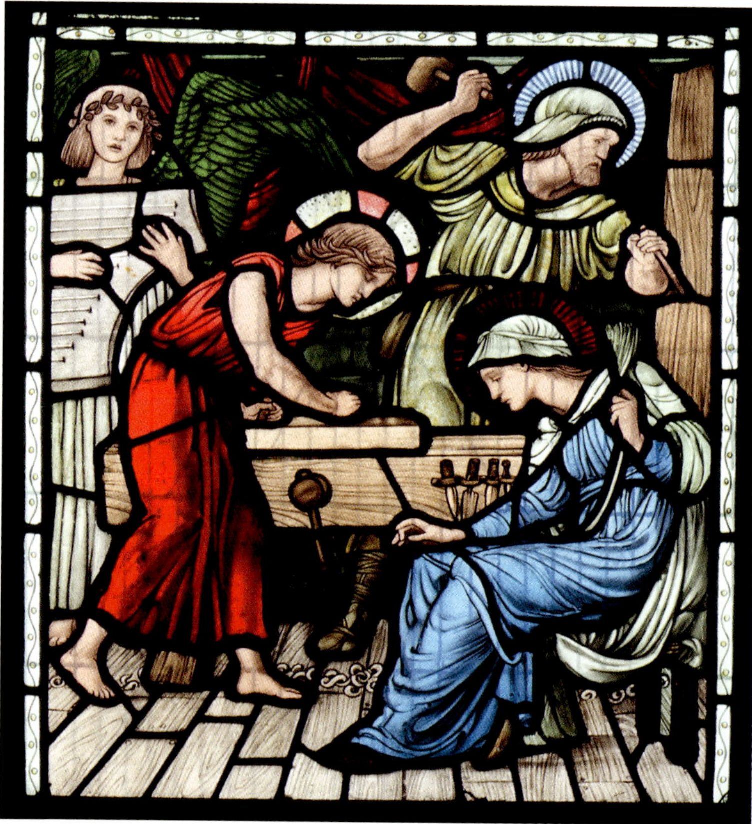

Christ the Carpenter from the chancel north window (west)

And in the next window we see where the Incarnation, 'the Word was made flesh and dwelt among us' (John 1:14), leads to. Jesus' ministry begins with his Baptism by John in the Jordan and the institution of Baptism. Alongside that there is the Last Supper and the institution of the Eucharist. Baptism and Eucharist are the two great dominical sacraments. In the former scene, Jesus stands in the river; the Baptist with his staff stands on the bank and the scene is observed by angels. In the upper room the heads are very close as the disciples ask 'Is it I?' So this scene is also about loyalty and betrayal. Notice the beloved disciple close to Jesus, echoing the place of Christ in relation to the Father (*see p. 60*). 'It is God the only Son, who is close to the Father's heart, who had made him known' (John 1:18).

Below, we have the small miracle of raising Lazarus from death, foretelling the great miracle of the Resurrection in the next window. In the former we see the sisters and Jesus calling to Lazarus emerging from his tomb (John 11). The burial of Jesus is depicted with a tenderness that is deeply moving. The dead Jesus is young and utterly vulnerable as he is carried by two disciples.

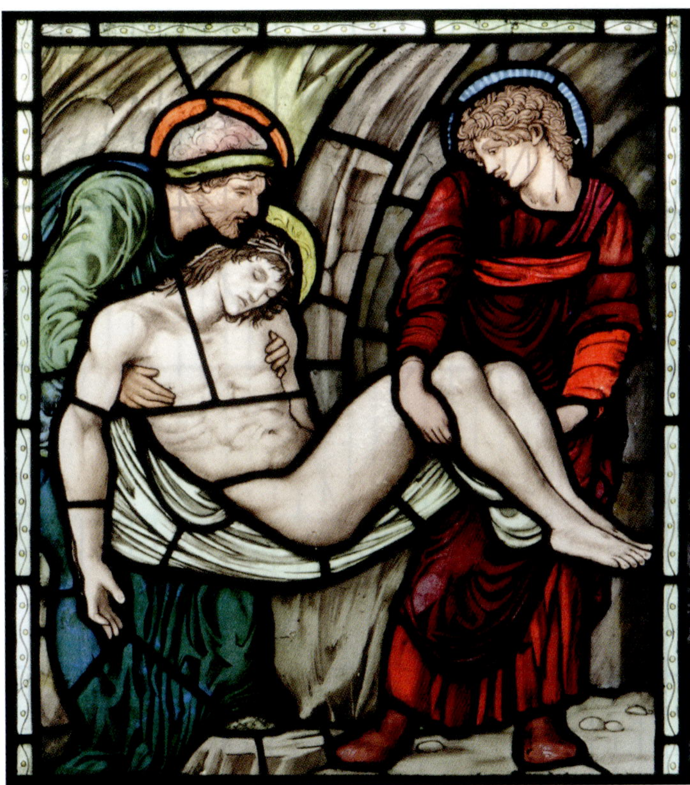

The Burial of Jesus from the chancel north window (east)

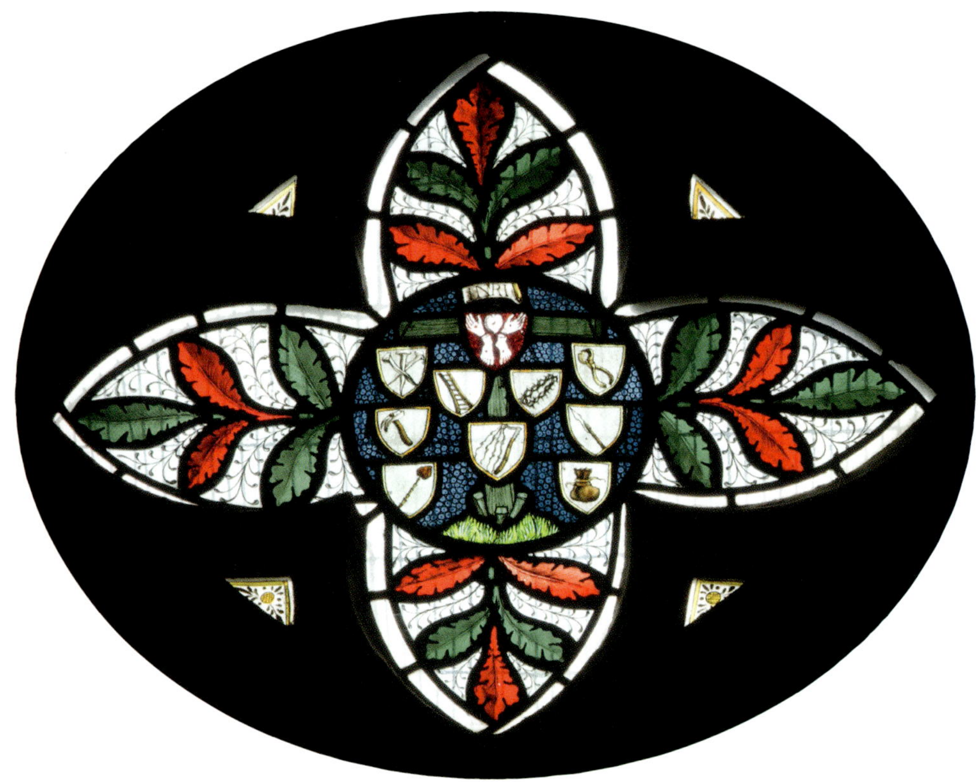

The Emblems of the Passion, from the top light of the chancel south window

Next we move to the window on the south side of the altar. The shields in the top quatrefoil and below are by Philip Webb; the two scenes are by Madox Brown. The coats of arms are of Sir Richard Sutton (*d.1524*) and William Smyth, Bishop of Lincoln (*d.1514*) who were the co-founders of Brasenose College, Oxford, in 1509. The College holds the patronage of Middleton Cheney.

There has been a long tradition of seeing an Old Testament event as fore-telling or paralleling in some way a New Testament one. This is known as type and antetype. It was first used in the writings of the Fathers of the Church, and throughout the later medieval period in paintings and glass as well as sermons and other writings. It had a renewal in the post-Reformation period, and was often used in Victorian glass. Here we have the type, but the antetype is left to us to read for ourselves – although we are given a strong hint in the quatrefoil shield with the emblems of the Passion, at the apex of the window. The left-hand scene is the sacrifice of Cain and Abel, the under-lying theology of sacrifice. On the right, Melchizedek offers bread and wine to Abraham. We are being invited to see the death of Jesus as a sacrifice.

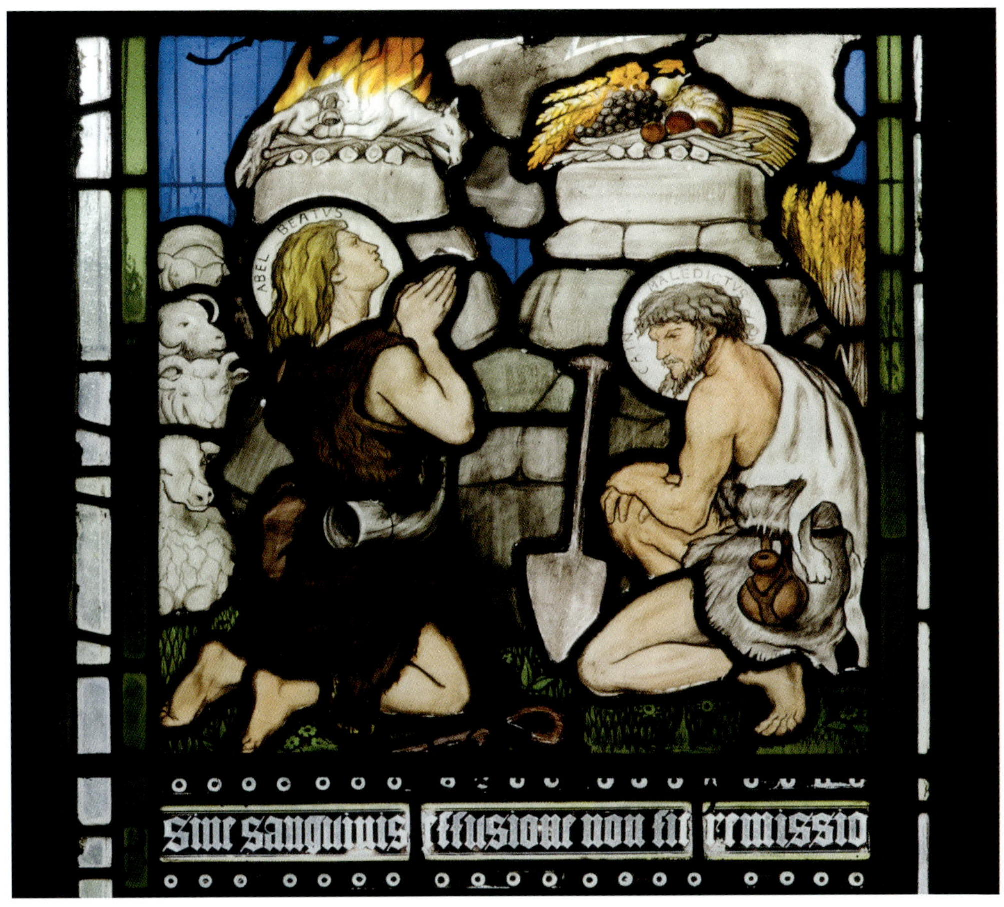

Cain and Abel, from the chancel south window

The two brothers have texts around their heads: *Abel beatus Cain maledictus* (blessed and cursed). The story in Genesis 4 tells of Abel offering a lamb from his flock and Cain the offerings of the ground. The Lord accepts Abel's sacrifice, but not that of Cain. We see this in the fire consuming the lamb, and in the attitudes of the two brothers. 'If you do not do well, sin is lurking at the door; its desire is for you, but you must master it': so Cain is addressed. And the story continues with the murder of Abel by Cain.

Melchizedek is the high priest of God and his story comes in Genesis 14. It is an extraordinary and mysterious story. Abram has rescued his nephew Lot from capture by a group of local kings. King Melchizedek of Salem brings out bread and wine. He is a priest of God Most High, we are told. And Abram gives Melchizedek one-tenth of everything. The name means 'king of righteousness', Salem means 'peace' and we can trace the biblical way of this figure: first in Psalm 110:4, God speaks to an earthly ruler and says, 'You are a priest for ever according to the order of Melchizedek'. Then in Hebrews 5:6 this psalm is cited (*see Hebrews 4:14– to the end of chapter 7 for the full reference*). The Letter to the Hebrews affirms that Christ is this priest, and makes much of Jesus as the true high priest entering the eternal holy of holies with his own blood. This makes a reality of the symbolic entry of the Jewish High Priest into the Holy of Holies of the Temple with the atoning blood of a sacrificial goat. But this passage in Hebrews is referring obliquely to the Crucifixion.

In the window you will notice the priestly garments, gold-slippered feet, a blue-lined, red cloak with morse (a metal clasp), a chasuble-type garment embroidered with lambs, and a fringed stole. In the late 1860s, when this window was made, these traditional Catholic vestments were beginning to be used again in the Church of England – and even if not actually in use, clerics were making a strong point in using them for biblical and angelic figures in the windows of their churches *(see p. 44)*.

Madox Brown makes his theological point with two biblical quotations from the Vulgate: Hebrews 9:22 – *Sine sanguinis fusione non fit remissio* ('without the shedding of blood there is no forgiveness'); and from Matthew 26:26 – *Accipite et comedite: hoc est corpus meum* ('Take and eat. This is my body.')

Is there any significance in the use of Latin texts? Probably not. Although common folk would not know any Latin, all educated people did; it was the staple of the grammar school.

So what doctrine of the Cross do we see here? It is oblique and therefore richer than a simple scene of the Cross would have been. This is theology rooted in the biblical. Jesus as the high priest, fulfilling in his passion and death the Old Testament's idea of sacrifice. Jesus' self-offering to the Father is the way of redemption. His sacrifice, like Abel's, is accepted by the Father. And this sacrifice is renewed in the offerings of the Eucharist.

SAINTS, APOSTLES, MARTYRS

The windows in the south aisle of the nave were not made by Morris & Co. These are by Powell and Sons of Whitefriars, the eastern window designed by J.W. Brown, and the western by G.W. Rhead. These two windows depict four Saints: (from the east) Luke, James, Andrew and John the Baptist.

The first window describes Luke as *medicus charissimus*, 'the beloved physician' as St Paul describes him in Colossians 4:14. The figure holds a large codex, clearly his writings, the Gospel and the book of Acts. The quarries have the letter L and inkhorns and quills, and there are acorns. In the borders we see crowns, shells, palms – and an ox, the symbol of Luke as Evangelist (Ezekiel 1:5ff and Revelation 4:6b–8).

On his right, St James *episcopus martyr* (bishop and martyr) also holds a clasped book and a club, the traditional instrument of his martyrdom. In the borders there is the mitre for a bishop and the letter J; which in Roman type looks like I.

St Andrew is described as Apostle and Martyr, the background quarries having palm leaves, symbols of martyrdom, and the saltire cross on which legend has it Andrew was crucified. The border has lilies, again symbols of purity. The text has *Invenimus Messiam* ('We have found the Messiah'), Andrew's words to Simon Peter in John 1:41, and *Salve Crux* ('Hail the Cross!')

St John the Baptist has the Cross with the resurrection banner. In the quarries we see the words: *Ecce Agnus Dei* ('Behold the Lamb of God!') from John 1:29. The Bible quotation continues: '... who takes away the sin of the world.' And it is the *Agnus Dei* of the Eucharist which has been used at the breaking of the Bread since at least the eighth century. We see also the words: *Vox clamantis in deserto* ('A voice crying in the wilderness'). This is the Baptist's reuse of words from Isaiah 40:3 which are quoted in Matthew 3:3, Mark 1:2, Luke 3:4 and John 1:23.

It is interesting that Andrew is described as Apostle, but James is described as Apostle and bishop. This latter reflects the teaching which the High Church tradition emphasised, that the bishops of the church are the successors of the Apostles – apostolic succession which enabled the laying on of hands to be traced back from the present bishops through the generations back to apostolic times. The continuance of this tradition had been a key in the Elizabethan and Restoration churches.

THE ADORATION OF THE LAMB

The inspiration for the great east window is from the book of Revelation. Chapter 5 records the adoration of the Lamb. Revelation 5:6 speaks of 'The Lamb looking as if it had been slaughtered, ... surrounded by the four living creatures, and the twenty-four elders.' The chapter describes many angels – myriads of myriads, '... and every creature in heaven and on earth and under the earth was singing: "To the one seated on the throne and to the Lamb be blessing and honour and glory and might for ever and ever."'

From the bottom to the top of the window there is movement, through the subtle use of colour and light. But 'earth' is seen in the light of heaven: the figures below are the redeemed.

Let us begin at the foot of the window: Abraham, Moses, Eve, Mary, Mary Magdalene, John, Agnes and Alban all show a story of faith, of the ethics of justice and mercy. Eve, the fallen one redeemed; Mary, the New Eve through whose obedience comes redemption; Mary Magdalene (also traditionally regarded as a fallen woman) healed and redeemed by Christ, appears with her jar of ointment with which to anoint the body of Jesus, a sign of her prodigious love and devotion. John, the beloved disciple and Apostle is shown with the Chalice and dragon. St Agnes was a young girl martyred in Rome who was steadfast in her devotion to Christ; and St Alban, the first martyr in Britain, who gave shelter to a priest, learnt the faith and died for refusing to burn incense to the emperor.

The second tier contains four Old Testament figures plus two from the New Testament and two from the early church. Adam is shown with boots and spade, Noah holds the Ark, David is crowned, with rich robes and the harp, and Isaiah has a flowering rod and a book. The rod refers to Isaiah 11:1 'a shoot shall come from the stem of Jesse' with reference to Isaiah's prophecy of the anointed one filled with gifts of the Holy Spirit, who would be descended from Jesse, the father of David. Peter and Paul, the two great Roman Saints who were both martyred in about AD65, have the traditional symbols of keys and a sword. Paul also has a scroll – the form his letters would have originally taken.

Then we have Austin, the common abbreviation for Augustine of Hippo, a great theologian and bishop, and St Catherine of Alexandria.

In the tier above them we see the Tribes of Israel with the words, 'And I heard the number of them which were sealed and there were sealed an hundred and forty and four thousand of all the tribes of the children of Israel.' This reflects on Revelation 7 in which John the Divine hears the number of those who are sealed and therefore saved from the terrible events that were to come. From each tribe 12,000 were sealed. So here we have the 12 tribes of Israel, each with a flag on which is a symbol. The symbols are derived from the blessings given by Jacob to his sons in Genesis 49. Jacob called to his sons, 'Gather around, that I may tell you what will happen to you in days to come'. Then addressing each one, from Reuben the first-born to Benjamin, he described their characteristics and something of their natures. And here in the window we see the symbols of those sayings on the flags.

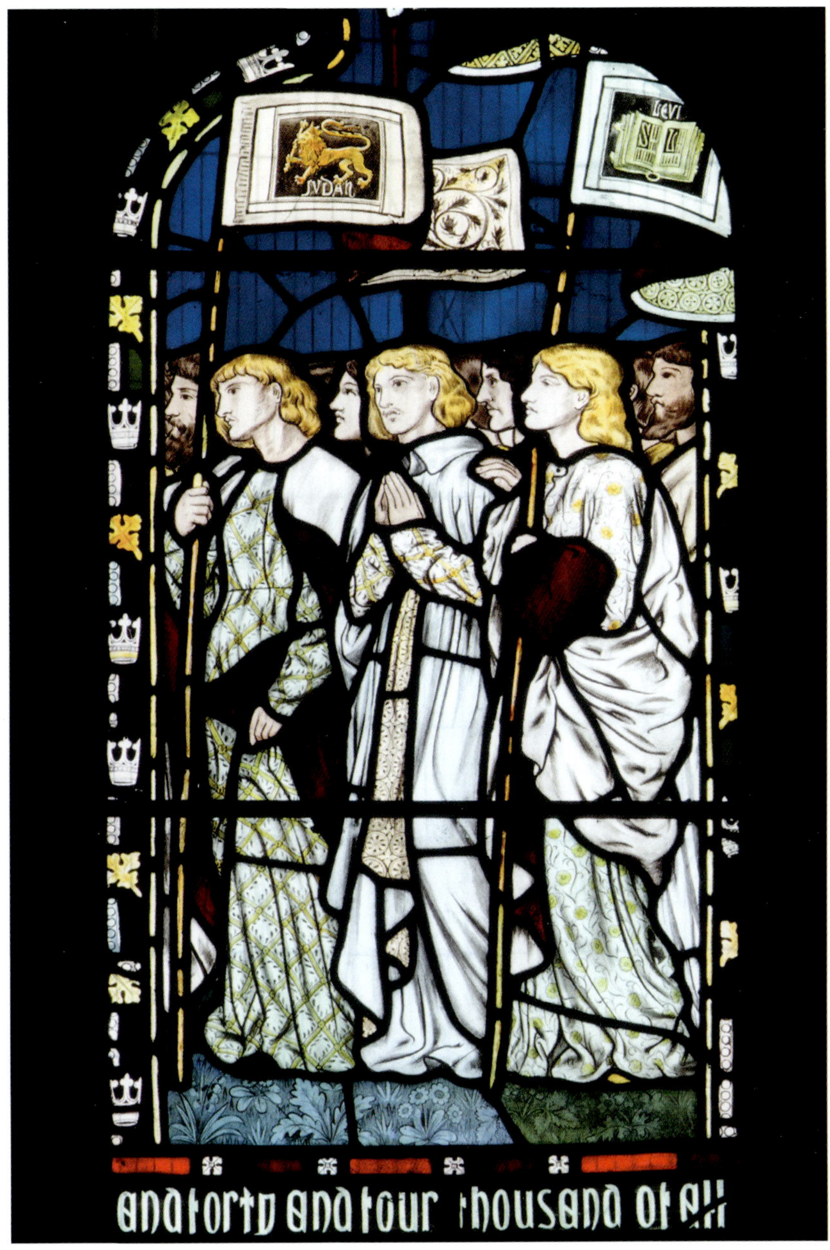

The Twelve Tribes of Israel from the east window (detail)

They are grouped in threes, and starting from the left side of the window we see: Gad a raider, Naphtali a goat, Asher rich food; then Benjamin a wolf, Zebulon a ship, Issacar a donkey. The third group is Judah a lion, Reuben unstable water and Levi a book. And then finally, Manasseh a palm branch,

Joseph a lamb and Simon a sword. You will notice that these figures look very un-Jewish: they are blond-haired and appear very English! However, they provide evidence of God's blessings and also the frailty of human living, for a lot of Jacob's remarks about his sons suggest violence and immorality. They also suggest the need of redemption in all of us, and remind us that the Saints below have reached the vision of God because they have been redeemed by Christ.

Above the Jewish tribesmen are the crowd of elders, the crystal sea and symbols of the four living creatures from Ezekiel and Revelation – Matthew the man, Mark the lion, Luke the ox and John the eagle. There are angels with censers (reminding us that there is much incense in the book of Revelation, *see Revelation 5:8 for example*) and these angels all wear albs and crossed stoles like priests.

As we look up at this window we are facing east, the place of sunrise and so of resurrection – the transcendent. We stand before the altar where the Eucharist is celebrated and where we eat the bread and drink the wine of Holy Communion. And we recall the words, 'Lift up your hearts ... Holy, holy, holy Lord God of hosts ... Lamb of God, you take away the sins of the world.'

One thing you may notice in these windows is that there is no image of the Crucifixion. The only references are in the Passion symbols in the south of the chancel. I think this is deliberate. In many churches the image of the dying or dead Christ predominates, and one can see why, for the death of Jesus is where God's love for the world is shown. But, of course, Christ is not dead, and it is therefore right that the image should be of resurrection.

BENEFACTORS AND MEMORIALS

In the east window we see the Communion of Saints, which is the whole company of believers living and departed. And our churches remind us of the many generations who have gone before us, many of them with memorials and graves. Some were benefactors and either gave things, like these windows, or have contributed to their maintenance. As we have seen there are coats of arms recording some of these connections: the Horton family and those connected with Brasenose College.

And so we return to the dove of the Holy Spirit descending, to give life to the people of God today.

Roger Bellamy, May 2017

Other Locations of Morris and Burne-Jones Stained Glass

In the autumn of 1865 (the year that Morris completed the commission for the east window at All Saints), he and his family moved from the Red House at Upton in the Kent countryside into a new workshop and living premises at 26 Queens Square, Bloomsbury. He was suffering from stress caused by overwork, financial problems with the business and rheumatic fever, so he was forced to eliminate the regular commute to Kent. These events were occurring at the same time that he was reaching the height of his personal artistic achievements in stained glass.

The firm of Morris & Co. had completed a number of important ecclesiastical commissions via the Gothic architect G.F. Bodley, a young friend of Morris, which helped to establish the firm's reputation. Amongst these were new-build Victorian church schemes at St Michael and All Angels, Brighton; Saint Martin, Scarborough and All Saints at Selsley in Gloucestershire. Morris's early commissions had all been for new churches; Middleton Cheney, however, was his first medieval church. Not long after the first window at Middleton Cheney, the firm also created stained glass locally for the church of Saint Mary, Bloxham. Llandaff Cathedral in Cardiff has a collection of windows designed by Morris and other Pre-Raphaelites and there are excellent examples of work by Burne-Jones at Jesus College Chapel, Cambridge. Upon completion of the Jesus College contract in 1878, Morris wrote to the College telling them, in his customary blunt fashion, that the firm would stop making stained glass for medieval churches, as he no longer approved of this type of restoration – so they were just in time.

BLOXHAM (ST MARY)

In 1864–66 the church was restored under the direction of the diocesan architect for Oxford, G.E. Street. Morris started an apprenticeship with Street in 1856, and moved from Oxford to London with the practice. In 1868 Burne-Jones created a stained glass window of St Christopher in the chancel at Bloxham, and in 1869 William Morris, Burne-Jones and Philip Webb created the east window. The church is located seven miles south west of Middleton Cheney.

BRIGHTON (ST MICHAEL AND ALL ANGELS)

Two churches in one: the first designed by architect G.F. Bodley and built in 1861–62 now forms just the south aisle of the current church. The second church was built because the first became outgrown, and was completed in 1893–95 to a design by William Burgess. The first church has glass by Morris; the second glass by Burne-Jones (including Burne-Jones' famous 'Flight into Egypt').

CAMBRIDGE (JESUS COLLEGE CHAPEL)

As part of the chapel restoration, Morris designed the painted roof of the nave, and completed the windows in the nave and transepts, to a design by Edward Burne-Jones of 1878.

CARDIFF (LLANDAFF CATHEDRAL)

A collection of six windows, designed by Morris in conjunction with Ford Madox Brown and Burne-Jones, and installed in 1866–70.

CODDINGTON (ALL SAINTS)

In a village to the east of Newark-on-Trent, Nottinghamshire. As part of a restoration by G.F. Bodley in 1864–65, Morris designed (and reputedly painted) a chancel ceiling of repeated patterns and Latin texts from the Psalms. New windows, which deserve comparison with Middleton Cheney, included a Crucifixion east window by Morris and Burne-Jones.

SCARBOROUGH (ST MARTIN)

An early French gothic style church, begun in 1861 by G.F. Bodley. All of the windows and much of the wall decoration is by Morris & Co. The recessed windows use both light and shadow, characteristic of the medieval period. The ten painted panels on the pulpit are particularly beautiful.

Another early French gothic style church designed by G.F. Bodley, this one of 1862. This was the first ecclesiastical commission for the firm of Morris & Co. The individual windows are by different members of the partnership, with the overall design probably by Webb. Following the medieval tradition – and in contrast to Middleton Cheney – the east window features the Crucifixion. The glass here is finely and richly coloured, and the church is frequently also visited by visitors to Middleton Cheney.

SOUTHGATE, NORTH LONDON (CHRIST CHURCH)

With London's affluent suburban expansion, the Weld Chapel on the Arnos Grove Estate proved inadequate. A new church, designed by George Gilbert Scott, was consecrated in 1862. This contains the largest collection of stained glass by Morris & Co in London, dating from 1861 to 1913, together with contemporaneous work by Clayton and Bell. Southgate represents an early encounter between Scott and Morris & Co. in design terms (perhaps even the first encounter).

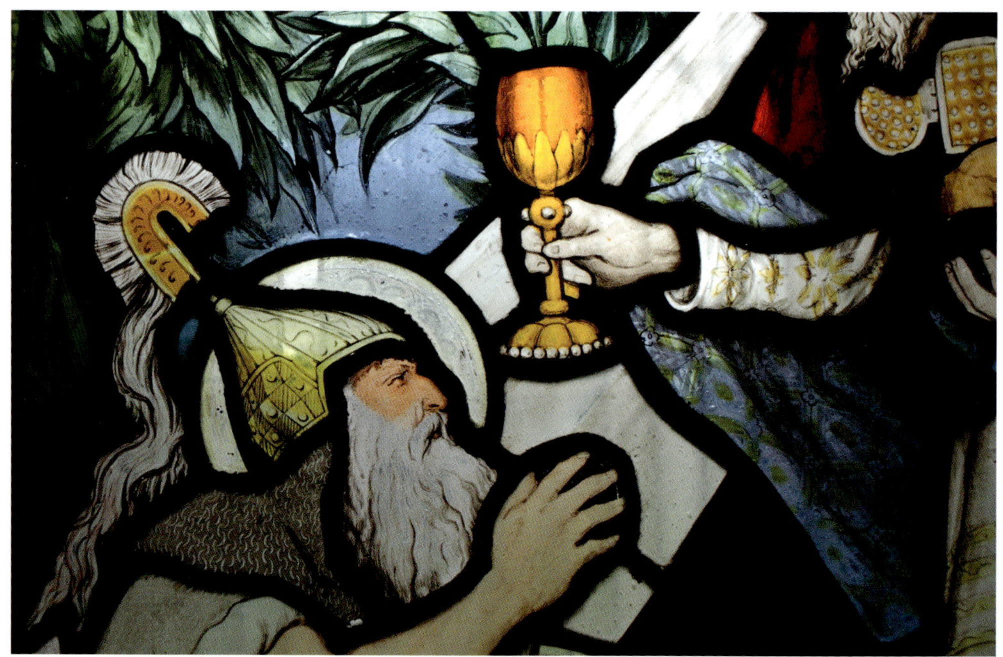

Detail from the chancel south window: Melchizedek and Abram

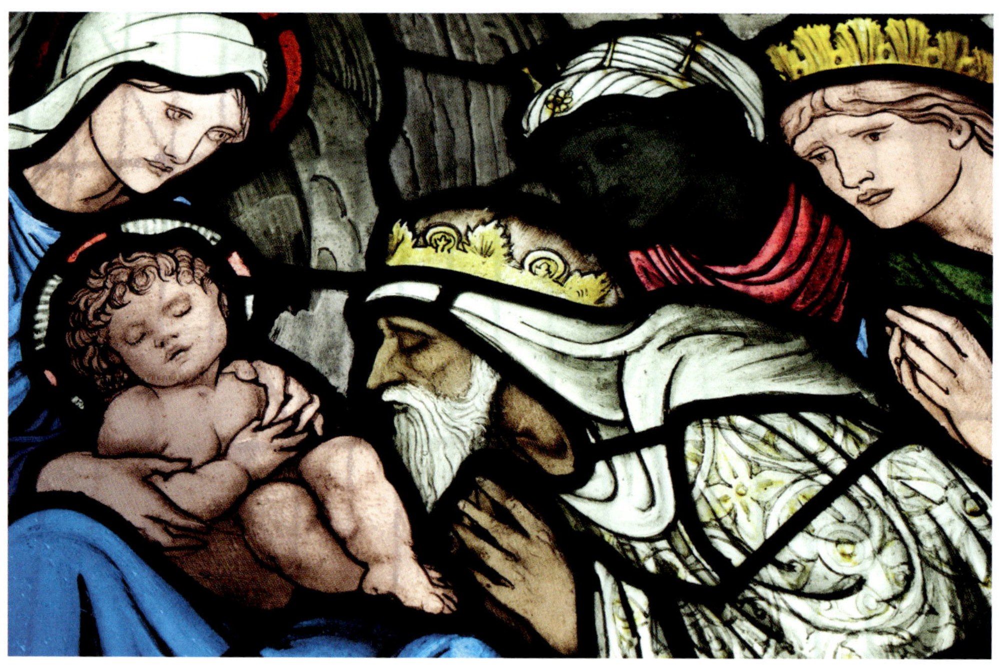

Detail from the chancel north window (w): The Adoration of the Magi

APPENDIX 2:
Select Bibliography

Bailey B., Pevsner N., & Cherry B., *Northamptonshire, The Buildings of England*, New Haven/ London, Yale University Press, 2013

Barringer, T., Rosenfeld, J. & Smith, A., *Pre-Raphaelites: Victorian Avant-Garde*, London, Tate Publishing, 2012

Coote S., *William Morris, His Life and Work*, Oxford, Past Times, 1995

Forrest, Irene, *Welcome to All Saints' Church Middleton Cheney* (church leaflet), 1994 (additions and amendments 2012–19)

Goodey, Brian, *William Morris Makes his Mark: The 1864 'Restoration' of All Saints Church, Middleton Cheney, Northants* (2020 forthcoming)

Hunter, Robert, *The Rebuilding of All Saints Church, Middleton Cheney from 1302* (church leaflet), 2007

— *William de Edington, Priest at Middleton Cheney* (church leaflet), 2018

Jenkins, S., *England's Thousand Best Churches*, London, Penguin Books, 2000

MacCarthy, F., *The Last Pre-Raphaelite: Edward Burne-Jones and the Victorian Imagination*, London, Faber and Faber, 2011

— *William Morris. A Life for Our Time*, London, Faber and Faber, 1994

Naylor, G. (ed.), *William Morris by Himself*, London, Little, Brown & Co., 1996

Sewter, A.C., *Middleton Cheney, Northants. All Saints* ('My Complete Catalogue Entries for the Church': typescript enclosed with letter to Professor N. Pevsner, 24:11:1960), Historic England Archive, 1960

— *The Stained Glass of William Morris and his Circle, Vol. 1*, New Haven/ London, Yale University Press for the Paul Mellon Centre for Studies in British Art, 1974

— *The Stained Glass of William Morris and his Circle, Vol. 2. A Catalogue*, New Haven/ London, Yale University Press for the Paul Mellon Centre for Studies in British Art, 1975

Sharpling, P., *Fragile Images. Post-medieval stained glass in Northamptonshire and the Stoke of Peterborough, Northampton*, Northamptonshire Record Society, 2016

Waters, W. & Carew-Cox, A., *Angels & Icons, Pre-Raphaelite Stained Glass 1850–1870*, Abbots Morton, Worcester, Seraphim Press, 2012

Website for All Saints Church, Middleton Cheney: www.allsaints-mc.church

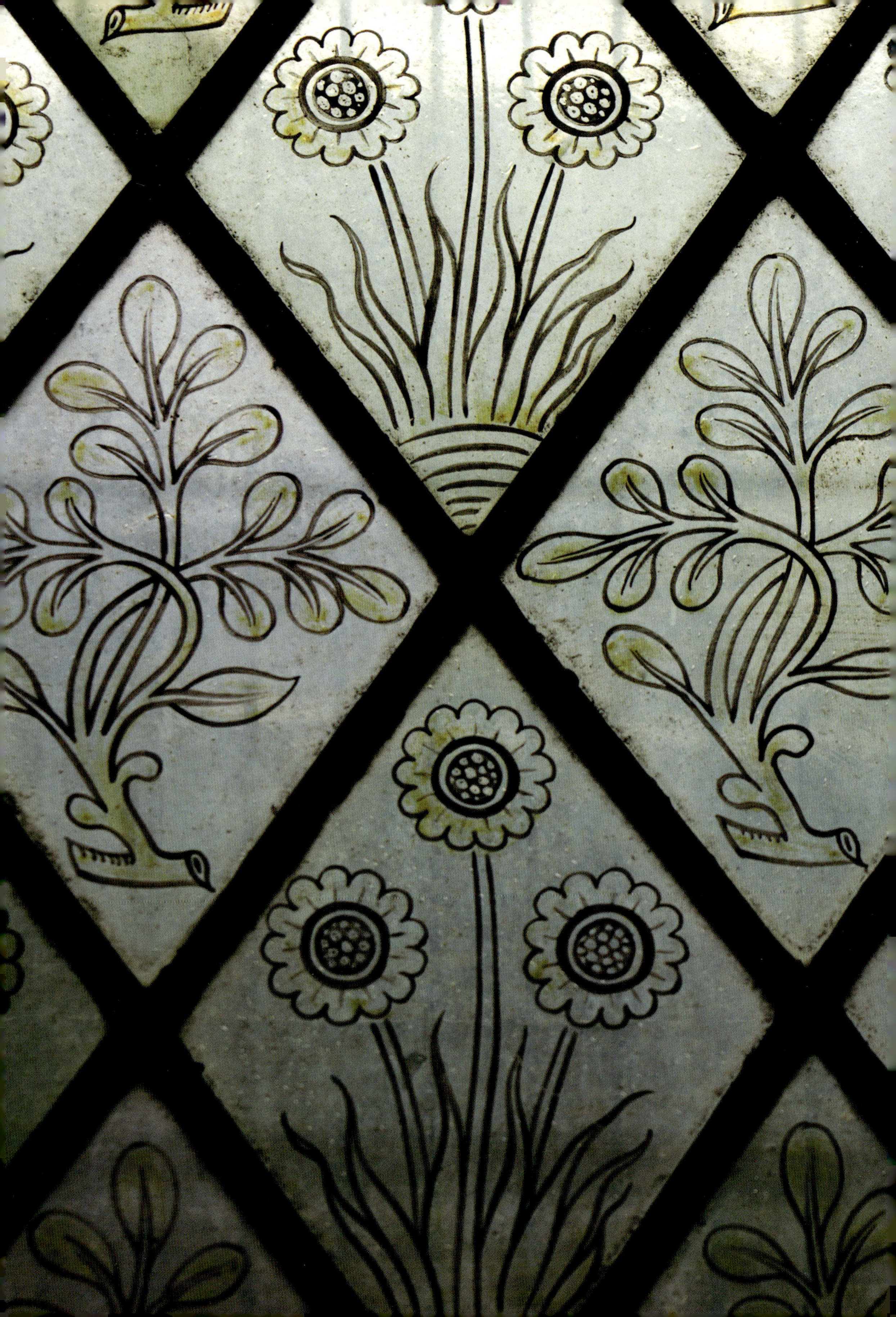